Havana, Cuba

Sam Night

Contents

Articles

Overview of Havana

Havana

Havana La Habana	
Ciudad de La Habana	

 **Flag** **Coat of arms**	
Nickname(s): *Ciudad de las Columnas* (Spanish) " City of Columns "	
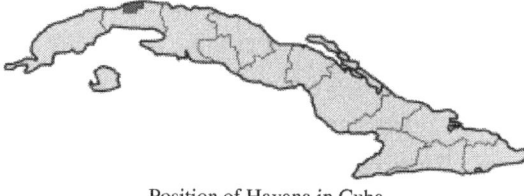 Position of Havana in Cuba	
Coordinates: 23°8′0″N 82°23′0″W	
Country	▨ Cuba
Province	Ciudad de La Habana

Founded	1515[a]
City status	1592
Founder	Diego Velázquez de Cuéllar
Municipalities	
Government	
- **Type**	Mayor-council
- **Body**	Ayuntamiento de La Habana
- **Mayor**	Juan Contino Aslán (PCC)
Area	
- **Total**	721 km^2 (278.4 sq mi)
Elevation	59 m (194 ft)
Population (2009)	
- **Total**	2,141,993
- **Density**	2970.8/km^2 (7694.3/sq mi)
Demonym	Havanan *habanero* (m), *habanera* (f)
Time zone	EST (UTC-5)
- **Summer (DST)**	EDT (UTC-4)
Postal code	10xxx-19xxx
Area code(s)	(+53) 7
[a] Founded on the present site was founded in **1519**.	

Havana (Spanish: ***La Habana***, pronounced [la a'βana] (listen), officially *Ciudad de La Habana*,) is the capital city, major port, and leading commercial centre of Cuba. The city is one of the 14 Cuban provinces. The city/province has 2.1 million inhabitants, the largest city in Cuba and the largest in the Caribbean region. The city extends mostly westward and southward from the bay, which is entered through a narrow inlet and which divides into three main harbours: Marimelena, Guanabacoa, and Atarés. The sluggish Almendares River traverses the city from south to north, entering the Straits of Florida a few miles west of the bay.

King Philip II of Spain granted Havana the title of City in 1592 and a royal decree in 1634 recognized its importance by officially designating it the "Key to the New World and Rampart of the West Indies". Havana's coat of arms carries this inscription. The Spaniards began building fortifications, and in 1553 they transferred the governor's residence to Havana from Santiago de Cuba on the eastern end of the island, thus making Havana the de facto capital. The importance of harbour fortifications was early recognized as English, French, and Dutch sea marauders attacked the city in the 16th century. The sinking of the U.S. battleship *Maine* in Havana's harbor in 1898 was the immediate cause of the Spanish-American War.

Present day Havana is the center of the Cuban government, and various ministries and headquarters of businesses are based there.

History

The founding of Havana

The current Havana area and its natural bay were first visited by Europeans during Sebastián de Ocampo's circumnavigation of the island in 1509. Shortly thereafter, in 1510, the first Spanish colonists arrived from Hispaniola and began the conquest of Cuba.

Conquistador Diego Velázquez de Cuéllar founded Havana on August 25, 1515 on the southern coast of the island, near the present town of Surgidero de Batabanó. Between 1514 and 1519, the city had at least two different establishments. All attempts to found a city on Cuba's south coast failed. The city's location was adjacent to a superb harbor at the entrance to the Gulf of Mexico, and with easy access to the Gulf Stream, the main ocean current that navigators followed when traveling from the Americas to Europe. This location led to Havana's early development as the principal port of Spain's New World colonies. An early map of Cuba drawn in 1514 places the town at the mouth of the River Onicaxinal, also on the south coast of Cuba. Another establishment was *La Chorrera*, today in the neighborhood of Puentes Grandes, next to the Almendares River.

Paseo del Prado

The final establishment, commemorated by El Templete, was the sixth town founded by the Spanish on the island, called *San Cristóbal de la Habana* by Pánfilo de Narváez: the name combines *San Cristóbal*, patron saint of Havana, and *Habana*, of obscure origin, possibly derived from *Habaguanex*, a native American chief who controlled that area, as mentioned by Diego Velasquez in his report to the king of Spain. A legend relates that *Habana* was the name of Habaguanex's beautiful daughter, but no known historical source corroborates this version. Others, such as the *Century Dictionary*, have connected it with the Middle Latin term *havana*, a derivation from the same Germanic word appearing in English as "haven". The English spelling of *Havana* was formerly **Havannah**, while ironically, the Spanish spelling of *Habana* was formerly *Havana*.

Havana moved to its current location next to what was then called *Puerto de Carenas* (literally, "Careening Bay"), in 1519. The quality of this natural bay, which now hosts Havana's harbor, warranted this change of location. Bartolomé de las Casas wrote:

> ...one of the ships, or both, had the need of careening, which is to renew or mend the parts that travel under the water, and to put tar and wax in them, and entered the port we now call Havana, and there they careened so the port was called *de Carenas*. This bay is very good and can host many ships, which I visited few years after the Discovery... few are in Spain, or elsewhere in the world, that are their equal...

Shortly after the founding of Cuba's first cities, the island served as little more than a base for the *Conquista* of other lands. Hernán Cortés organized his expedition to Mexico from the island. Cuba, during the first years of the Discovery, provided no immediate wealth to the conquistadores, as it was poor in gold, silver and precious stones, and many of its settlers moved to the more promising lands of Mexico and South America that were being discovered and colonized at the time. The legends of Eldorado and the Seven Cities of Gold attracted many adventurers from Spain, and also from the adjacent colonies, leaving Havana and the rest of Cuba largely unpopulated.

Pirates and *La Flota*

Havana was originally a trading port, and suffered regular attacks by buccaneers, pirates, and French corsairs. The first attack and resultant burning of the city was by the French corsair Jacques de Sores in 1555. The pirate took Havana easily, plundering the city and burning much of it to the ground. De Sores left without obtaining the enormous wealth he was hoping to find in Havana. Such attacks convinced the Spanish Crown to fund the construction of the first fortresses in the main cities — not only to counteract the pirates and corsairs, but also to exert more control over commerce with the West Indies, and to limit the extensive *contrabando* (black market) that had arisen due to the trade restrictions imposed by the *Casa de Contratación* of Seville (the crown-controlled trading house that held a monopoly on New World trade).

To counteract pirate attacks on galleon convoys headed for Spain while loaded with New World treasures, the Spanish crown decided to protect its ships by concentrating them in one large fleet, which would traverse the Atlantic Ocean as a

Real Fuerza Fortress

El Morro Fortress

group. A single merchant fleet could more easily be protected by the Spanish Armada. Following a royal decree in 1561, all ships headed for Spain were required to assemble this fleet in the Havana Bay. Ships arrived from May through August, waiting for the best weather conditions, and together, the fleet departed Havana for Spain by September.

This naturally boosted commerce and development of the adjacent city of Havana (a humble *villa* at the time). Goods traded in Havana included gold, silver, alpaca wool from the Andes, emeralds from Colombia, mahoganies from Cuba and Guatemala, leather from the Guajira, spices, sticks of dye from Campeche, corn, manioc, and cocoa. Ships from all over the New World carried products first to Havana, in order to be taken by the fleet to Spain. The thousands of ships gathered in the city's bay also fueled Havana's agriculture and manufacture, since they had to be supplied with food, water, and other products needed to traverse the ocean. In 1563, the *Capitán General* (the Spanish Governor of the island) moved his residence from Santiago de Cuba to Havana, by reason of that city's newly gained wealth and importance, thus unofficially sanctioning its status as capital of the island.

On December 20, 1592, King Philip II of Spain granted Havana the title of City. Later on, the city would be officially designated as "Key to the New World and Rampart of the West Indies" by the Spanish crown. In the meantime, efforts to build or improve the defensive infrastructures of the city continued. The San Salvador de la Punta castle guarded the west entrance of the bay, while the Castillo de los Tres Reyes Magos del Morro guarded the eastern entrance. The Castillo de la Real Fuerza defended the city's center, and doubled as the Governor's residence until a more comfortable palace was built. Two other defensive towers, La Chorrera and San Lázaro were also built in this period..

17th-18th Centuries

Havana expanded greatly in the 17th century. New buildings were constructed from the most abundant materials of the island, mainly wood, combining various Iberian architectural styles, as well as borrowing profusely from Canarian characteristics. During this period the city also built civic monuments and religious constructions. The convent of St Augustin, El Morro Castle, the chapel of the Humilladero, the fountain of Dorotea de la Luna in La Chorrera, the church of the Holy Angel, the hospital of San Lazaro, the monastery of Santa Teresa and the convent of San Felipe Neri were all completed in this era.

In 1649 a fatal epidemic brought from Cartagena in Colombia, affected a third of the population of Havana. On November 30, 1665, Queen Mariana of Austria, widow of King Philip IV of Spain, ratified the heraldic shield of Cuba, which took as its symbolic motifs the first three castles of Havana: the Real Fuerza, the Tres Santos Reyes Magos del Morro and San Salvador de la Punta. The shield also displayed a symbolic golden key to represent the title "Key to the Gulf". On 1674, the works for the City Walls were started, as part of the fortification efforts. They would be completed by 1740.

By the middle of the 18th century Havana had more than seventy thousand inhabitants, and was the third largest city in the Americas, ranking behind Lima and Mexico City but ahead of Boston and New

York.

British occupation

Further information: Great Britain in the Seven Years War

The city was captured by the British during the Seven Years' War. The episode began on June 6, 1762, when at dawn, a British fleet, comprising more than 50 ships and a combined force of over 11,000 men of the Royal Navy and Army, sailed into Cuban waters and made an amphibious landing east of Havana. The invaders seized the heights known as La Punta on the east side of the harbor and commenced a bombardment of nearby El Morro Castle, as well as the city itself. After a two month siege, El Morro was attacked and taken only after dying the brave defender Luis Vicente de Velasco e Isla, on 30 July 1762. The city formally surrendered on 13 August. It was subsequently governed by Sir George Keppel on behalf of Great Britain. Although the British only lost 560 men to combat injuries during the siege, more than half their forces ultimately died due to illness, yellow fever in particular.

The British immediately opened up trade with their North American and Caribbean colonies, causing a rapid transformation of Cuban society. Food, horses and other goods flooded into the city, and thousands of slaves from West Africa were transported to the island to work on the undermanned sugar plantations. Though Havana, which had become the third largest city in the new world, was to enter an era of sustained development and strengthening ties with North America, the British occupation was not to last. Pressure from London by sugar merchants fearing a decline in sugar prices forced a series of negotiations with the Spanish over colonial territories. Less than a year after Havana was seized, the Peace of Paris was signed by the three warring powers thus ending the Seven Years' War. The treaty gave Britain Florida in exchange for the city of Havana on the recommendation of the French, who advised that declining the offer could result in Spain losing Mexico and much of the South American mainland to the British.

After regaining the city, the Spanish transformed Havana into the most heavily fortified city in the Americas. Construction began on what was to become the Fortress of San Carlos de la Cabaña, the biggest Spanish fortification in the New World. The work extended for eleven years and was enormously costly, but on completion the fort was considered an unassailable bastion and essential to Havana's defence. It was provided with a large number of cannons forged in Barcelona. Other fortifications were constructed, as well: the castle of *Atarés* defended the Shipyard in the inner bay, while the castle of *El Príncipe* guarded the city from the west. Several cannon batteries located along the bay's canal (among them the *San Nazario* and *Doce Apóstoles* batteries) ensured that no place in the harbor remained undefended.

Paseo del Prado leading to Parque Central

The Havana cathedral was constructed in 1748 as a Jesuit church, and converted in 1777 into the *Parroquial Mayor* church, after the Suppression of the Jesuits in Spanish territory in 1767. In 1788, it formally became a Cathedral. Between 1789 and 1790 Cuba was apportioned into an individual diocese by the Roman Catholic Church. On January 15, 1796, the remains of Christopher Columbus were transported to the island from Santo Domingo. They rested here until 1898, when they were transferred to Seville's Cathedral, after Spain's loss of Cuba.

Centro Habana district

Havana's shipyard (named *El Arsenal*) was extremely active, thanks to the lumber resources available in the vicinity of the city. The *Santísima Trinidad* was the largest warship of her time. Launched in 1769, she was about 62 meters long, had three decks and 120 cannons. She was later upgraded to as many as 144 cannons and four decks. She sank following the Battle of Trafalgar in 1805. This ship cost 40.000 *pesos fuertes* of the time, which gives an idea of the importance of the Arsenal, by comparing its cost to the 26 million *pesos fuertes* and 109 ships produced during the Arsenal's existence.

Centro Habana district

19th century

As trade between Caribbean and North American states increased in the early 19th century, Havana became a flourishing and fashionable city. Havana's theaters featured the most distinguished actors of the age, and prosperity amongst the burgeoning middle-class led to expensive new classical mansions being erected. During this period Havana became known as the Paris of the Antilles.

Museo de la Revolución

The 19th century opened with the arrival in Havana of Alexander von Humboldt, who was impressed by the vitality of the port. In 1837, the first railroad was constructed, a 51 km stretch between Havana and Bejucal, which was used for transporting sugar from the valley of Guinness to the harbor. With this, Cuba became the fifth country in the world to have a railroad, and the first Spanish-speaking country. Throughout the century, Havana was enriched by the construction of additional cultural facilities, such as the Tacon Teatre, one of the most luxurious in the world, the Artistic and Literary Liceo (Lyceum) and the theater Coliseo.

In 1863, the city walls were knocked down so that the metropolis could be enlarged. At the end of the century, the well-off classes moved to the quarter of Vedado. Later, they emigrated towards Miramar, and today, evermore to the west, they have settled in Siboney. At the end of the 19th century, Havana witnessed the final moments of Spanish colonialism in America, which ended definitively when the United States warship *Maine* was sunk in its port, giving that country the pretext to invade the island. The 20th century began with Havana, and therefore Cuba, under occupation by the USA. In 1906 the Bank of Nova Scotia opened the first branch in Havana. By 1931 it had three branches in Havana.

Republican period and Post-revolution

During the Republican Period, from 1902 to 1959, the city saw a new era of development. All endeavors of industry and commerce grew very rapidly. Cuba recovered from the devastation of war to become a well-off country, with the third largest middle class in the hemisphere, and Havana, the Capital of the country, became known as the Paris of the Caribbean. Construction was an important industry. Apartment buildings to accommodate the new middle class, as well as mansions for the Cuban tycoons, were built at a fast pace. Numerous luxury hotels, casinos and nightclubs were constructed during the 1930s to serve Havana's burgeoning tourist industry, strongly rivaling Miami. In the thirties, organized crime characters were not unaware of Havana's nightclub and casino life, and they made their inroads in the city. Santo Trafficante, Jr. took the roulette wheel at the Sans Souci, Meyer Lansky directed the Hotel Habana Riviera, Lucky Luciano, the Hotel Nacional Casino, and the Havana Hilton owned by the Hospitality Workers Retirement Fund was Latin America's tallest, largest hotel. At the time Havana became an exotic capital of appeal and numerous activities ranging from marinas, grand prix car racing, musical shows and parks. The spectacular development and opportunity offered by Cuba in general and Havana in particular, made the island a magnet for immigration. Cuba received millions of immigrants from all corners of the world during the Republic. It received so many Spaniards that today it is estimated that one quarter of the Cuban population descends from Spanish immigrants.

Havana achieved the title of being the Latin American city with the biggest middle class population per-capita simultaneously accompanied by gambling and corruption where gangsters and stars were known to mix socially. During this era, Havana was generally producing more revenue than Las Vegas, Nevada. A gallery of black and white portraits from the era still adorn the walls of the bar at the Hotel National, including pictures of Frank Sinatra with Ava Gardner, Marlene Dietrich and Gary Cooper. In 1958, about 300,000 American tourists visited the city. One of the most well-known visitors and resident to the area was the American author Ernest Hemingway (1899–1961), who quoted "*in terms of beauty, only Venice and Paris surpassed Havana*", Hemingway wrote several of his famous novels in Cuba and lived there the last 22 years of his life. Havana had 135 cinemas at that time — more than Paris or New York City.

After the revolution of 1959, the new regime promised to improve social services, public housing, and official buildings; nevertheless, shortages that affected Cuba after Castro's abrupt expropriation of all private property and industry under a strong communist model backed by the Soviet Union followed by the U.S. embargo, hit Havana especially hard. As a result, today much of Havana is in a dilapidated state. By 1966-68, the Cuban government had nationalized all privately owned business entities in Cuba, down to "certain kinds of small retail forms of commerce" (law No. 1076). Most of these laws and economic restrictions still remain today. Havana and Cuba in general transformed from an immigrant receiver, to one the largest emigration generators in the world. Today almost 15% of the total Cuban population lives abroad, even despite the fact that free travel is banned by the regime.

There was a severe economic downturn after the collapse of the Soviet Union in 1991 and with it the end of the billions of dollars in subsidies the Soviet Union gave the Cuban government, with many believing Havana's soviet backed regime would soon vanish, as it happened to the Soviet satellite states of Eastern Europe. However, contrary to the soviet satellite states of Eastern Europe, Havana's communist regime prevailed during the 1990s. The worsening situation has been illustrated by the favorite joke in the summer of 1991. Soon after Fidel Castro came to power, the signs in the Havana Zoo were changed from "don't feed the animals" to "don't eat the animal's food". During the Special Period, the signs begged visitors not to eat the animals. Indeed, the peacocks, the buffalo and even the rhea reportedly disappeared from the Havana zoo.

After 50 years of prohibition, the communist government increasingly turned to tourism for new financial revenue, and has allowed foreign investors to build new hotels and develop hospitality industry. Paradoxically, while foreign investment is welcome, Cubans are forbidden to participate. The Cuban population is only allowed to work as cooks, gardeners and taxi-drivers, but not to become owners or investors of any property. For these reason among others, the tourism industry during the socialist revolution has failed to generate the projected revenues. After a decline in the early 2000s, Cuban tourism hit an all time high of 2.7 billion dollars (USD) in

An old American car in a typical street view of Havana in 2010

2008. An effort has also gone into rebuilding Old Havana for tourist purposes and a number of streets and squares have been rehabilitated. But Old Havana is a large city, and the restoration efforts concentrate in all but less than 10% of its area.

Geography

The city extends mostly westward and southward from the bay, which is entered through a narrow inlet and which divides into three main harbours: Marimelena, Guanabacoa, and Atarés. The sluggish Almendares River traverses the city from south to north, entering the Straits of Florida a few miles west of the bay. The low hills on which the city lies rise gently from the deep blue waters of the straits. A noteworthy elevation is the 200-foot- (60-metre-) high limestone ridge that slopes up from the east and culminates in the heights of La Cabaña and El Morro, the sites of colonial fortifications overlooking the bay. Another notable rise is the hill to the west that is occupied by the University of Havana and the Prince's Castle.

Climate

Havana, like much of Cuba, enjoys a pleasant year-round tropical climate that is tempered by the island's position in the belt of the trade winds and by the warm offshore currents. Under the Köppen climate classification, Havana has a tropical savanna climate. Average temperatures range from 72 °F (22 °C) in January and February to 82 °F (28 °C) in August. The temperature seldom drops below 50 °F (10 °C). The lowest temperature was 33 °F (1 °C) in Santiago de Las Vegas, Boyeros. The lowest recorded temperature in Cuba was 32 °F (0 °C) in Bainoa, Havana province. Rainfall is heaviest in June and October and lightest from December through April, averaging 46 inches (1200 mm) annually. Hurricanes occasionally strike the island, but they ordinarily hit the south coast, and damage in Havana is normally less than elsewhere in the country.

On the night of July 8–9, 2005, the eastern suburbs of the city took a direct hit from Hurricane Dennis, with 100 mph (160 km/h) winds. The storm whipped fierce 10-foot (3.0 m) waves over Havana's seawall, and its winds tore apart pieces of some of the city's crumbling colonial buildings. Chunks of concrete fell from the city's colonial buildings. At least 5,000 homes were damaged in Havana's surrounding province. Three months later, in October 2005, the coastal regions suffered severe flooding following Hurricane Wilma. The table below lists temperature averages throughout the year:

Climate data for Havana

Month	Jan	Feb	Mar	Apr	May	Jun	Jul	Aug	Sep	Oct	Nov	Dec	Year
Average high °C (°F)	25.8 (78.4)	26.1 (79)	27.6 (81.7)	28.6 (83.5)	29.8 (85.6)	30.5 (86.9)	31.3 (88.3)	31.6 (88.9)	31.0 (87.8)	29.2 (84.6)	27.7 (81.9)	26.5 (79.7)	28.8 (83.8)
Average low °C (°F)	18.6 (65.5)	18.6 (65.5)	19.7 (67.5)	20.9 (69.6)	22.4 (72.3)	23.4 (74.1)	23.8 (74.8)	24.1 (75.4)	23.8 (74.8)	23.0 (73.4)	21.3 (70.3)	19.5 (67.1)	21.6 (70.9)
Rainfall mm (inches)	64.4 (2.535)	68.6 (2.701)	46.2 (1.819)	53.7 (2.114)	98.0 (3.858)	182.3 (7.177)	105.6 (4.157)	99.6 (3.921)	144.4 (5.685)	180.5 (7.106)	88.3 (3.476)	57.6 (2.268)	1189.2 (46.819)
% Humidity	75	74	73	72	75	79	78	78	79	80	77	75	76.3
Avg. rainy days (≥ 1.0 mm)	5	5	3	3	6	10	7	9	10	11	6	5	80

Source: World Meteorological Organisation (UN), Climate-Charts.com

City layout

Contemporary Havana can essentially be described as three cities in one: Old Havana, Vedado, and the newer suburban districts. Old Havana, with its narrow streets and overhanging balconies, is the traditional centre of part of Havana's commerce, industry, and entertainment, as well as being a residential area.

To the north and west a newer section, centred on the uptown area known as Vedado, has become the rival of Old Havana for commercial activity and nightlife. Centro Habana, sometimes described as part of Vedado, is mainly a shopping district that lies between Vedado and Old Havana. The Capitolio Nacional marks the beginning of Centro Habana, a working class neighborhood. Chinatown and the Real Fabrica de Tabacos Partagás, one of Cuba's oldest cigar factories is located in the area.

A third Havana is that of the more affluent residential and industrial districts that spread out mostly to the west. Among these is Marianao, one of the newer parts of the city, dating mainly from the 1920s. Some of the suburban exclusivity was lost after the revolution, many of the suburban homes having been nationalized by the Cuban government to serve as schools, hospitals, and government offices. Several private country clubs were converted to public recreational centres. Miramar located west of

Vedado along the coast, remains Havana's exclusive area; mansions, foreign embassies, diplomatic residences, upscale shops, and facilities for wealthy foreigners are common in the area. The International School of Havana is located in the Miramar neighborhood.

In the 1980s many parts of Old Havana, including the Plaza de Armas, became part of a projected 35-year multimillion-dollar restoration project. The government sought to instil in Cubans an appreciation of their past and also to make Havana more enticing to tourists in accordance with the government's effort to boost tourism and thus increase foreign exchange. In the past ten years, with the assistance of foreign aid and under the support of local city historian Eusebio Leal Spengler, large parts of Habana Vieja have been renovated. The city is moving forward with their renovations, with most of the major plazas (Plaza Vieja, Plaza de la Catedral, Plaza de San Francisco and Plaza de Armas) and major tourist streets (Obispo and Mercaderes) near completion.

Architecture

Neo-classical

Havana is unique due to its unrivalled rhythmic arcades built largely by Spanish immigrants. Many interior patios remain similar to designs in Seville, Cadiz and Granada. Neo-classicism affected all new buildings in Havana and can be seen all over the city. Many urban features were introduced into the city at the time including Gas public lighting in 1848 and the railroad in 1837. In the second half of the 18th century, sugar and coffee production increased rapidly, which became essential in the development of Havana's most prominent architectural style. Many wealthy *Habaneros* took their inspiration from the French; this can be seen within the interiors of upper class houses such as the *Aldama Palace* built in 1844. This is considered the most important neoclassical residential building in Cuba and typifies the design of many houses of this period with portales of neoclassical columns facing open spaces or courtyards. The railway terminal (1912), the University of Havana, (1906–1940) and the Capitolio (1926–1929) are also neo-classical buildings. The Capitolio dome was at 62 meters the highest point in the city, inspired by the USA Capitol building.

Great Theatre of Havana

Cathedral of Havana

In 1925 Jean-Claude Nicolas Forestier, the head of urban planning in Paris moved to Havana for five years to collaborate with architects and landscape designers. In the master planning of the city his aim was to create a harmonic balance between the classical built form and the tropical landscape. He embraced and connected the city's road networks while accentuating prominent landmarks. His influence has left a huge mark on Havana although many of his ideas were cut short by the great depression in 1929. During the first decades of the 20th century Havana expanded more rapidly than at any time during its history. Great wealth prompted architectural styles to be influenced from abroad. The peak of Neoclassicism came with the construction of the Vedado district (begun in1859). This whole neighbourhood is littered with set back well-proportioned buildings.

Lonja del Comercio

El Capitolio

Colonial and Baroque

Great riches were brought from the colonialists into and through Havana as it was a key transshipment point between the new world and old world. As a result Havana was the most heavily fortified city in the Americas. Most examples of early architecture can be seen in military fortifications such as La Fortaleza de San Carlos de la Cabana (1558–1577) designed by Juan Antonelli and the Castillo del Morro (1589–1630). This sits at the entrance of Havana Bay and provides an insight into the supremacy and wealth at that time. Old Havana was also protected by a defensive wall begun in 1674 but had already overgrown its boundaries when it was completed in 1767, becoming the new neighbourhood of Centro Habana.

"Malecon" avenue in Vedado

The influence from different styles and cultures can be seen in Havana's colonial architecture, with a diverse range of Moorish, Spanish, Italian, Greek and Roman. The Convento de Santa Clara (1638 - 18th century) is a good example of early Spanish influenced architecture. Its great hall resembles an inverted ship and shows the skill of early craftsmen. The Havana cathedral (1748–1777) dominating the Plaza de la Catedral (1749) is the best example of Cuban Baroque. Surrounding it are the former palaces of the Count de Casa-Bayona (1720–1746) Marquis de Arcos (1746) and the Marquis de Aguas Claras (1751–1775).

Art Nouveau, Art Deco and Eclectic

At the turn of the 20th century Havana, along with Buenos Aires, was the grandest and most important Latin American city in terms of architecture. This boom period known as *vacas gordas* (fat cows) demonstrates huge examples of buildings from the international influences of art nouveau, art deco and eclectic. Its suburbs developed to what we see today as Miramar, Marianao, Vedado and Playa. The lush and wealthy Miramar was set out on the American street grid pattern and became a home to diplomats and foreigners. The Lopez Serrano building built in 1932 by Ricardo Mira was the first tall building in Cuba and inspired by the Rockefeller Center in New York. Its design influence can be seen in many buildings in Miami and Los Angeles. The Edificio Bacardi (1930) is one of Havana's grandest buildings and its best example of Art Deco. Located on a small knoll overlooking the entrance to Havana Bay, is the art-deco style Hotel Nacional de Cuba; originally built in 1929-30 through a joint agreement with the Cuban government and U.S.-based bank.

Modernism

Havana, like Las Vegas in the 40s and 50s, developed from marketing itself as a destination for gambling and holidays in the sun. Many high-rise office buildings, and apartment complexes, along with some hotels built in the 1950s dramatically altered the skyline. Modernism, therefore, transformed much of the city and should be noted for its individual buildings of high quality rather than its larger key buildings. Examples of the latter are Habana Libre (1958), which before the revolution was the Havana Hilton Hotel and La Rampa movie theater (1955). Famous architects such as Walter Gropius, Richard Neutra and Oscar Niemeyer all passed through the city while strong influences can be seen in Havana at this time from Le Corbusier and Ludwig Mies van der Rohe.

The Edificio Focsa (1956) represents Havana's economic dominance at the time. This 35-story complex was conceived and based on Corbusian ideas of a self-contained city within a city. It contained 400 apartments, garages, a school, a supermarket, and restaurant on the top floor. This was the tallest concrete structure in the world at the time (using no steel frame) and the ultimate symbol of luxury and excess. The Havana Riviera Hotel (1957) designed by Irving Feldman, a twenty-one-story, 440-room edifice, towering above the Malecon in Havana was another angular and futuristic building build on the Vedado area impressive for its era. When it opened, the Riviera was the largest purpose-built casino-hotel in Cuba or anywhere in the world, outside Las Vegas (the Havana Hilton (1958) surpassed its size a year later). It was owned by the *Caja de Retiro Gastronómico* (Hospitality Workers retirement Fund) to equal the comfort and contemporary luxury of any Las Vegas hotel of the era. Jose Luis Sert had also designed an artificial island off the Malecón whose construction was planned to take place in the 1960s. It was to incorporate huge modern towers, hotels, casinos, and shopping centers which would cater for the city's growing tourism. This like many other post-1959 projects never materialized.

Landmarks

- **Fortaleza San Carlos de la Cabaña**, a fortress located on the east side of the Havana bay, La Cabaña is the most impressive fortress from colonial times, particularly its walls constructed (at the same time as El Morro) at the end of the 18th century.

- **El Capitolio Nacional**, built in 1929 as the Senate and House of Representatives, this colossal building is recognizable by its dome which dominates the city's skyline. Inside stands the third largest indoor statue in the

The landmark Russian Embassy.

  world, *La Estatua de la República*. Nowadays, the Cuban Academy of Sciences headquarters and the Museo Nacional de Historia Natural (the National Museum of Natural History) has its venue within the building and contains the largest natural history collection in the country.

- **Castillo de los Tres Reyes Magos del Morro** is a picturesque fortress guarding the entrance to Havana bay, constructed because of the threat to the harbor from pirates.

- **Castillo San Salvador de la Punta**, a small fortress built in the 16th century, at the western entry point to the Havana harbour, it played a crucial role in the defence of Havana during the initial centuries of colonisation. The fortress still houses some twenty old guns and other military antiques.

- **El Cristo de La Habana**, Havana's statue of Christ blesses the city from the other side of the bay, much like the famous Cristo Redentor in Rio de Janeiro. Carved from marble by Jilma Madera, it was erected in 1958 on a platform which makes a good spot from which to watch old Havana and the harbor.

- **The Great Theatre of Havana**, famous particularly for the acclaimed National Ballet of Cuba, it sometimes hosts performances by the National Opera. The theater is also known as concert hall, García Lorca, the biggest in Cuba.

- **Hotel Nacional de Cuba**, Art Deco National Hotel.

- **El Malecón Habanero**, the avenue that runs beside the seawall built along the northern shore of Havana, from Habana Vieja to the Almendares River, it forms the northern boundary of Old Havana, Centro Habana and Vedado.

- **Museo de la Revolución**, located in the former Presidential Palace, with the yacht Granma on display behind the museum.

- **Necrópolis Cristóbal Colón**, a cemetery and open air museum, it is one of the most famous cemeteries in Latin America, known for its beauty and magnificence. The cemetery was built in 1876 and has nearly one million tombs. Some of the gravestones are decorated with the works of sculptors of the calibre of Ramos Blancos, among others.

Coat of arms

Main article: Seal of Havana

Culture

Havana, by far the leading cultural centre of the country, offers a wide variety of features that range from museums, palaces, public squares, avenues, churches, fortresses (including the largest fortified complex in the Americas dating from the 16th through 18th centuries), ballet and from art and musical festivals to exhibitions of technology. The restoration of Old Havana offered a number of new attractions, including a museum to house relics of the Cuban revolution. The government placed special emphasis on cultural activities, many of which are free or involve only a minimal charge.

Before the Communists, Havana cinema rivalled New York City and Paris. As Guillaume Carpentier put it in a Le Monde article, "with nationalisation, they closed one by one, for lack of maintenance, films or electricity... Havana, Cubans complain, is a cemetery of cinemas. It is also a cemetery of bookshops, markets, shops..."

Parque Central

Old Havana

Main article: Old Havana

In Old Town Havana.

Old Havana, (*La Habana Vieja* in Spanish), contains the core of the original city of Havana, it is the richest colonial set of Latin America. Havana Vieja was founded by the Spanish in 1519 in the natural harbor of the Bay of Havana. It became a stopping point for the treasure laden Spanish Galleons on the crossing between the New World and the Old World. In the 17th century it was one of the main shipbuilding centers. The city was built in baroque and neoclassic style. Many buildings have fallen in ruin but a number are being restored. The narrow streets of old Havana contain many buildings, accounting for perhaps as many as one-third of the approximately 3,000 buildings found in Old Havana.

Old Havana is the ancient city formed from the port, the official center and the Plaza de Armas. Alejo Carpentier called Old Havana the place "de las columnas" (of the columns). The Cuban government is taking many steps to preserve and to restore Old Havana, through the Office of the city historian, directed by Eusebio Leal. Old Havana and its fortifications were added to the UNESCO World Heritage List in 1982.

Chinatown

Further information: Chinese Cuban

Havana's Chinatown (Barrio Chino), once Latin America's largest and most vibrant Chinatown incorporated into the city by the early part of the 20th century when hundreds of thousands of Chinese workers were brought in by Spanish settlers from Guangdong, Fujian, Hong Kong, and Macau during the following decades to replace and / or work alongside African slaves. After completing 8-year contracts or otherwise obtaining their freedom, many Chinese immigrants settled permanently in Havana. The Chinatown neighborhood was booming with Chinese restaurants, laundries, banks, pharmacies, theaters and several Chinese-language newspapers, the neighborhood comprised 44 square blocks during its prime. The heart of Havana's Chinatown is on *el Cuchillo de Zanja* (or The Zanja Canal). The strip is a pedestrian-only street adorned with many red lanterns, dancing red paper dragons and other Chinese cultural designs, there is a great number of restaurants that serve a full spectrum of Chinese dishes - unfortunately that 'spectrum' is said by many not to be related to real Chinese cuisine.

Havana's Chinatown district. The paifang (arch) is located on Dragones street.

Ballet Nacional de Cuba during a performance in the Great Theater of Havana

The Chinatown district has two paifang, a large one located on *Calle Dragones*, the materials were donated in the late 90s by the People's Republic of China, it has a well defined written welcoming sign in Chinese and Spanish. The smaller arch is located on Zanja strip. The Cuban's Chinese boom ended when Fidel Castro's 1959 revolution seized private businesses, sending tens of thousands of business-minded Chinese fleeing, mainly to the United States. Descendants are now making efforts to preserve and revive the culture.

Only one of what were once four Chinese-language newspapers remains in Havana, *Kwong Wah Po*, written by Abel Fung, member of the Promotional Group of Chinatown. The newspaper is not subject to state censorship. To tie in with the Revolution's economic reliance on tourism, attempts have recently been launched to attract revitalization investment for Chinatown from state-run enterprises of the People's Republic of China and overseas Chinese private investors, particularly Chinese Canadians. In addition, Chinatown is today the only area granted autonomy from many laws that govern the rest of Cuba. Restaurants, for example, are not state run nor are they subject to the laws of private restaurants in that they are allowed to have more than 12 seats as well as serve seafood.

Visual arts

A small palace located on 17th Street and E, is the very well maintained neo-classical mansion of the *Countess of Revilla de Camargo*, today it is the Museum of Decorative Arts (*Museo de Artes Decorativas*), known as the *small French Palace of Havana* built between 1924 and 1927, it was designed in Paris by architects P. Virad and M. Destuque, inspired in French Renaissance. A lavish display of 18th and 19th century European treasures that recall a time when Havana was known as *the Paris of the Antilles*, and many luxury goods, including porcelain from Worcester, Meissen and Sèvres, were imported.

In the French room, a marble bust of Marie Antoinette smiles demurely, her graceful neck intact. There is another room full of Chinese screens, another one featuring English furniture and landspcape painting. For more than 40 decades the museum has been exhibiting more than 33,000 works dating from the reigns of Louis XV, Louis XVI, and Napoleon III; as well as 16th to 20th century Oriental pieces, among many other treasures. The Museum has ten permanent exhibit halls with works that range from the 16th to the 20th centuries. Among them are prominent porcelain articles from the factories in Sèvres and Chantilly, France; Meissen, Germany; and Wedgwood, England, as well as Chinese from the *Kien Lung* period and Japanese from the Imari. The furniture comes from Leonard Boudin, SimoneauWikipedia:WikiProject Disambiguation/Fixing links, Jean Henri Riesener and several others.

The National Museum of Fine Arts is a Fine Arts museum that exhibits Cuban art collections from the colonial times up to contemporary generation. There are two impressive buildings, one dedicated to Cuban Art and the Universal Art, in the former *Asturian Center*, the former Fine Arts Museum built in 1954 is dedicated exclusively to housing Cuba Art collections. Several museums in Old Havana contain furniture, silverware, pottery, glass and other items from the colonial period. A great one of these is the Palace of the General Captains, where Spanish governors once lived. The Casa de Africa presents another aspect of Cuba's history, an impressive collection of Afro-Cuban religious artifacts.

The Museo Nacional de Bellas Artes containing works by Rubens, Goya and Velazquez is now closed for renovations; it is open to public at a temporary location on Calle Trocadero until renovations are complete. Other museums includes Casa de los Árabes and the Casa de Asia with Middle and Far Eastern collections. Many of these small boutiques museums are in elegant old Spanish architecture houses with airy courtyards. The Museo de Finanzas is more than an empty vault where dictator Fulgencio Batista once stashed his loot. A few old bank-notes are displayed on the walls. Havana's *Museo del Automobil* has an impressive collection of vehicles dating back to a 1905 Cadillac. In the Automobile museum there is also a Rolls Royce which belonged to Batista, near the 1960 Chevrolet that Che Guevara drove.

The Museum of the Revolution (*Museo de la Revolución*), designed in Havana by Cuban architect Maruri, and the Belgian Jean Beleu, who came up with an eclectic design, harmoniously combines Spanish, French and German architectural elements. The museum was the Presidential Palace; today, its displays and documents outline Cuba's history from the beginning of the *neo-colonial period*. While most museums of Havana are situated in Old Havana, few of them can also be found in Vedado. In total, Havana has around 50 museums, including the Museum of Fine Art, the Revolution and Decorative Arts; the National Museum of Music; the Museum of Dance and Rum; the Cigar Museum; the Napoleonic, Colonial and Oricha Museums; the Museum of Anthropology; the Ernest Hemingway Museum; the José Martí Monument; the Aircraft Museum (Museo del Aire). There are also museums of Natural Sciences, the City, Archeology, Gold-and-Silverwork, Perfume, Pharmaceuticals, Sports, Numismatics, and Weapons.

Performing arts

After the sun sets, Havana's performing arts come to life. Facing the Central Park is the baroque Great Theatre of Havana, a prominent theatre built in 1837. It is now home of the National Ballet of Cuba and the International Ballet Festival of Havana, one of the oldest in the New World and remarkably was once the most technologically advanced in the world, thanks to the Italian scientist, Antonio Meucci.

Meucci's ingenious spirit lives on in the theatre. Located in the *Paseo de Prado* in a building known as the *Palacio del Centro Gallego*. The façade of the building is adorned with a stone and marble statue. There are also sculptural pieces by Giuseppe Moretti, representing allegories depicting benevolence, education, music and theatre. The principal theatre is the García Lorca Auditorium, with seats for 1,500 and balconies. Glories of its rich history; the Italian tenor Enrico Caruso sang, the Russian ballerina Anna Pavlova danced, and the French Sarah Bernhardt acted.

Another grand theatre is the National Theater of Cuba, housed in a huge modern building, decorated with works by Cuban artists. There are two main theatre stages, the Avellaneda hall and the Covarrubias hall, as well as a smaller theatre workshop space on the ninth floor. The Karl Marx Theater is the venue has an enormous auditorium with seating capacity of 5500 people, and is generally used for big shows by stars from Cuba and abroad. The theatre is also a major concert venue for both local and international artists; singer-songwriters such as Carlos Varela, Silvio Rodríguez and Pablo Milanés, are just a few of the famous artists who have graced this particular stage. More recently, this was the scene of a concert by British pop group The Manic Street Preachers.

Festivals

Cuban International Jazz Festival

Many festivals held in Cuba are centered around the arts such as music, dance, art, and even film making. One of these such festivals is the annual Cuban International Jazz Festival which was founded by many well known Cuban jazz musicians which includes Cuba's infamous Bobby Carcasses (the very well known Afro-Cuban jazz "Havana Jazz Festival." The very first venue for this jazz concert was the

Casa de La Cultura Plaza in downtown Havana which is still home to many music and jam sessions that take place to this very day. Based on the festival's booming success the concert has extended to include all the main concert halls in downtown Havana, not to mention the spontaneous street jam sessions that that take place outside of these halls. The event features artists that come from all over the world including Argentina, Chile, the United States (in the past), and many other countries who come to celebrate their love of jazz with other enthusiasts.

The International Havana Ballet Festival

The International Havana Ballet Festival (Festival Internacional de Ballet de La Habana) is among one of the most prestigious international events dedicated to elevating the art of dance. Created in 1960 by a joint effort of the Ballet Nacional de Cuba, the Instituto Nacional de la Industria Turística and the cultural organizations of the government, the International Ballet Festival of Havana was added to the plans of massive diffusion of arts started after the popular Cuban Revolution on January 1, 1959. The Festival, with its character, has allowed people to enjoy the performances and the works of prestigious figures of the world of the dance and has also shown to the visitors the high level reached by the Cuban ballet. This Festival, which currently is held in alternate years, is the oldest of its kind worldwide, and meets at different venues in the Cuban capital and in other cities, big stars of the dance companies, personalities Highlights in the history of ballet, as well as critics, journalists and entrepreneurs. El evento no tiene carácter competitivo y su objetivo es el encuentro fraternal de artistas y otros especialistas en aras del arte, la amistad y la paz. The event is non competitive and its objective is the fraternal meeting of artists and other specialists for the sake of art, friendship and peace. Every two years the Havana International Ballet festival draws packed houses of Cuban and foreign dance enthusiasts and critics.As one of the biggest and best-loved events of its kind in the country, the International Ballet Festival of Havana attracts some of the most prestigious dancers from around the world who perform along with artists from the country's own National Ballet of Cuba. The first ever International Ballet Festival of Havana was held in 1960 and became a biannual event from 1974. To this day, the event continues to be one of the most prominent ballet festivals in Cuba and attracts audiences from all over the globe.

Havana's International Film Festival

As one of the most well-known Cuban festivals, Havana's International Film Festival was founded on December 3, 1979 as a way to pay tribute and give a voice to Spanish-language film makers because they were not well represented during that time. As a tradition, the festival takes place every December in the city of Havana, Cuba. The event organizes several contests in sections of interest, such as fiction medium and short length films, first timers, documentary, animation, scripts and posters, though the major attraction of the whole event is the Official Section Contest, in which some 21 feature films aspire to win the Coral Award, the Oscar of the Festival. The festival is the starting place for many now mainstream films such as the critically acclaimed movie "City of God" which was Brazil's official film submission for the festival in 2002 which was a 1970's action melodrama that follows a young photographer's emotional and professional development as he hovers on the outskirts of gang action.

Las Parrandas de Remedios Festival

One of the oldest festivals in Cuba takes place in Remedios, Cuba (outside of Havana) which is distinguished by many Cubans for its Christmas festival, "Las Parrandas de Remedios", one of the most popular events of the region that takes place between the 16th to the 26th of December every year. Considered the oldest festivities in Cuba, the "parrandas" were initially promoted by Father Francisco Vigil de Quiñones, who used to officiate at the Iglesia Mayor of San Juan Bautista de los Remedios. The priest, who was concerned about the absence of parishioners at the "Misa de Gallo" (midnight mass), had the idea of encouraging children to take to the streets and wake up the citizens using whistles, horns and tin cans, so that they had no other choice than get up and attend mass. That singular and noisy initiative got deeply rooted among the population, resulting in the most attractive festivity in the country. In 1871, the "parrandas" adopted a structure that has survived the passage of time. According to tradition, when the bells of the Iglesia Parroquial Mayor (Major Parochial Church) toll at 9 o'clock on the night of December 24, two neighborhoods make public their creativeness and efforts made during the entire year to participate in the competition. During the "parrandas", a "fierce" competition takes place between the neighborhoods of San Salvador, represented by the colors red and blue, and a rooster as a symbol, and El Carmen, represented by the color brown and a globe. The memory of those celebrations is compiled at the Museum of Parrandas, which opened in a 19th century building in 1980 in Remedios, where photos, documents and hand-made objects linked to the festivities are preserved.

Habanos Cigar Festival

Every year Havana plays host to the Habanos Cuban Cigar Festival in the month of February. The festival has been in existence since its start in 1997 by Habanos S.A. who is the company whom controls the promotion, distribution, and export of Cuban cigars and other tobacco products worldwide and actually holds 70% of the global market outside of the U.S. The festival is usually held within a five day time span where activities during the festival include: tours of the cigar factories, a trade fair, various seminars focused on the production, distribution and history of Havanos cigars, cigar tastings, Habanosommelier contest, an instruction class on how to roll a Habano, and visits to tobacco plantations. Attendees of this event include exclusive distributors, "La Casa del Habano" managers from all over the world, production and sales executives, producers and marketers of luxury and smoker products, tobacco producers, dealers of the tobacco industry , artisans and collectors, smoker clubs, amateur smokers, and Habano lovers.

Economy

Industry

Havana's economy first developed on the basis of its location, which made it one of the early great trade centres in the New World. Sugar and a flourishing slave trade first brought riches to the city, and later, after independence, it became a renowned resort. Despite efforts by Fidel Castro's government to spread Cuba's industrial activity to all parts of the island, Havana remains the centre of much of the nation's industry. The traditional sugar industry, upon which the island's economy has been based for three centuries, is centred

Chinese cargo ship leaving the harbour

elsewhere on the island and controls some three-fourths of the export economy. But light manufacturing facilities, meat-packing plants, and chemical and pharmaceutical operations are concentrated in Havana. Other food-processing industries are also important, along with shipbuilding, vehicle manufacturing, production of alcoholic beverages (particularly rum), textiles, and tobacco products, particularly the world-famous Habanos cigars. Although the harbours of Cienfuegos and Matanzas, in particular, have been developed under the revolutionary government, Havana remains Cuba's primary port facility; 50% of Cuban imports and exports pass through Havana. The port also supports a considerable fishing industry.

Following the collapse of the Soviet Union in 1991 and the United States embargo against Cuba, Havana and the rest of Cuba suddenly plunged into its worst economic crisis since before the 1959 Revolution, the crisis was known officially as the Special Period in Time of Peace. The effects of the Special Period and consequent food shortages have had greatest repercussions in the city of Havana. In addition to the decline in food production needed to serve the capital, there is also a shortage of petroleum necessary to transport, refrigerate, and store food available from the rural agricultural sector. Havana has been designated as a priority in the National Food Program; urban gardening has figured critically among the many measures taken to enhance food security. After the collapse of the Soviet Union, Cuba re-emphasized tourism as a major industry leading to its recovery. Tourism is now Havana and Cuba's primary economic source.

Tourism

Before the Cuban Revolution – and particularly from 1915 to 1930 - tourism was one of Cuba's major sources of hard currency (behind only the sugar and tobacco industries). Havana, where a kind of laissez-faire attitude in all things leisurely was the norm, was the Caribbean's most popular destination, particularly with US citizens, who sought to skirt the restrictions of American prohibition.

Following a severe drop in the influx of tourists to the island (resulting, primarily, from the Great Depression, the end of prohibition in the United States and the outbreak of World War II), Havana began to welcome visitors in significant numbers again in the 1950s, when US organized crime secured control of much of the leisure and tourism industries in the country. This was a time when Cuba's foreign minister boasted that Havana spent as much on parties as any major capital in the world, when the island was the mob's most secure link in the drug-trafficking chain which culminated in the United States and when the country's justified reputation for sensuality and dolce vita pursuits earned it the appellation of "the Latin Las Vegas". Meyer Lansky built the Hotel Riviera [1], Santo TrafficanteWikipedia:WikiProject Disambiguation/Fixing links came to own shares in the Sevilla and a casino was opened at the Hotel Plaza [2] during this time.

It was tourism's association to the world of gambling and prostitution which made the revolutionary government established in 1959 approach the entire sector as a social evil to be eradicated. Many bars and gambling venues were closed down following the revolution and a government body, the National Institute of the Tourism Industry, took over many facilities (traditionally available to wealthy) to make them accessible to the general public.

With the deterioration of Cuba − US relations and the imposition of a trade embargo on the island in 1961, tourism dropped drastically and did not return to anything close to its pre-revolution levels until 1989. The revolutionary government in general, and Fidel Castro in particular, initially opposed any considerable development of the tourism industry, linking the sphere to the debauchery and criminal activities of times past. In the late 1970s, however, Castro changed his stance and, in 1982, the Cuban government passed a foreign investment code which opened a number of sectors, tourism included, to foreign capital.

Through the creation of firms open to such foreign investment (such as Cubanacan [3], established in 1987), Cuba began to attract capital for hotel development, managing to increase the number of tourists from 130,000 (in 1980) to 326,000 (by the end of that decade).

As a result of the collapse of the Soviet Union and its Eastern European allies in 1989 and early 90s, Cuba was plunged into a severe economic crisis and saw itself in desperate need of foreign currency. The answer, again, was found in tourism, and the Cuban government spent considerable sums in the industry to attract visitors. Following heavy investment, by 1995, the industry had become Cuba's main source of income.

Commerce and finance

After the Revolution, Cuba's traditional capitalist, American dominated, free-enterprise system was replaced by a heavily socialized economic system. The majority of business in Cuba is in the hands of the state. In Havana Cuban-owned businesses and U.S.-owned businesses were nationalized and today most businesses operate solely under state control. In Old Havana and throughout Vedado there are a several small private businesses, such as shoe-repair shops or dressmaking facilities, but their number is steadily declining. Banking as well is also under state control, and the National Bank of Cuba, headquartered in Havana, is the control center of the Cuban economy. Its branches in some cases occupy buildings that were in pre-revolutionary times the offices of Cuban or foreign banks.

Vedado is today Havana's financial district, the main banks, airline companies offices, shops, most businesses headquarters, numerous high-rise apartments and hotels, are located in the area. In the late 1990s Vedado, located along the Caribbean waterfront, started to represent the principal commercial area. It was developed extensively between 1930 and 1960, when Havana developed as a major destination for U.S. tourists; high-rise hotels, casinos, restaurants, and upscale commercial establishments, many reflecting the art deco style. The University of Havana is located in Vedado.

Transportation

Transport

Further information: Transportation in Cuba

Havana was renowned for an excellent network of public transportation by bus and taxi. A subway system modeled after that of New York City was even proposed in 1921. In 1959, Havana's buses carried out over 29,000 daily bus trips across a dense layout of routes that connected the 600,000 inhabitants of Havana. After the Socialist Revolution, all business were nationalised, and public transport was assigned to the Ministerio del Transporte (MITRANS). In the Province of the City of Havana, Provincial Transport Authority functions are carried out by 11 divisions. But this bureaucratic, complex system of central control produces today only 8,000 trips per day, for a population that triples that of 1959.[*citation needed*]

Former EMT Valencia bus now serving in Havana

Public transport must be self-financing. Until 1994, general government funds from MITRANS (of around $US4 million per annum) were used to fund the Provincial Transport Directorate in the City of Havana budget. Public transport in Havana has always been able to cover operating expenses that are paid in Cuban Pesos through the fares. But there has been a constant problem with financing fuel, new vehicles and spare parts and other supplies which require hard currency

British Ford Anglia in Havana

like US dollars – which led to a reduction in service provision. To address this, enterprises that generate hard currency (like the tourist taxis, tourist rental cars, and tourist cocotaxi elements of Panatrans and the Transmetro services that hire out buses and trucks to dollar-owning companies) cross subsidise the other services, in particular OM and MetroBus.

In addition, a service planning team from the Regional Transit Authority of Paris (RATP) has been working to redefine the public transport network in the capital. The main aim of this project has been to rationalise the number of existing routes to match the actual passenger demand. The first of these new principal routes has already been put into place.

Air

Havana was the destination of the first international flight carried by a US airline: in 1927 Juan Trippe's Pan-American World Airways flew from Key West, Florida to Havana. In 1946, a Cuban pioneer named Reinaldo Ramirez, started a route, the first from Latin America to Europe, that flew from Havana to Madrid, Spain. The ship was named "La Ruta de Colon", and the company name was "Aerovías Cubanas internacionales" Havana is served by José Martí International Airport. It lies about 11 km south of the city center, and is the main hub of Cubana de Aviación. José Martí International Airport is Cuba's main international and domestic getaway, it is also hub of Aerogaviota and Aero Caribbean. The airport serves several million passengers each year, 80% of Cuba's international passengers along with Varadero's Airport, it handles flights from over 25 international airlines serving more than 60 worldwide destinations, mainly in Europe, North, Central and South America and over 3 national airlines serving 16 domestic destinations. Havana is also served by Playa Baracoa Airport which is small airport to the west of city used for some domestic flights, primarily Aerogaviota. Cuban passengers are required to obtain a permit from the authorities to leave the island, know as the White Card, and those Cubans living abroad are required a visa to enter their own country.

Rail

Havana has a network of suburban, interurban and long-distance rail lines, the only one in the Caribbean region. The railways are nationalised and run by the UFC (Union de Ferrocarriles de Cuba – Union for Railways of Cuba). Rail service connects Havana from the *Central Rail Station*, *La Coubre'* and *Casablanca stations* to various Cuban provinces. Currently annual passenger volume is some 12 million, but demand is estimated at two-and-a-half to three times this value, with the busiest route being between Havana and Santiago de Cuba, some 836 km apart by rail. In 2000 the Union de Ferrocarriles de Cuba bought French first class airconditioned coaches.

Fast trains line 1 and 2 between Havana (Central Station) and Santiago de Cuba use comfortable stainless-steel air-conditioned coaches bought from French Railways and now known as "el tren francés" (the French train). It runs daily at peak periods of the year (Summer season, Christmas & Easter), and on every second day at other times of the year. These coaches were originally used on the premier Trans Europ Express service between Paris, Brussels and Amsterdam before being replaced with high speed Thalys trains. They were shipped to the Cuban Railways System in 2001. It offers two classes of seating, basic leatherette "especial" and quite luxurious "primera especial".

Bus

The Havana public buses are carried out by two divisions, Omnibus Metropolitanos (OM) and MetroBus. The Omnibus Metropolitanos division has one of the most used and largest urban bus fleets in the country, its fleet is widely diverse in new and old donated bus models, primerally well used Busscar Urbanuss manufactured by Mercedes-Benz with an additional new 255 purchased in 2004. and the infamous camellos (camels), which are truck trailers ill-fitted for passenger transportation. The Cuban government will invest millions of dollars for the acquisition of 1,500 new Yutong urban buses and another 1,000 interprovincial buses in a 5 years period, which unfortunately will not cover the demand of transportation services. There are several inter-province bus services such as *Astro*, the regular National public transportation, Astro connects the capital city with all over the island, in 2005 Astro completely replaced its fleet with brand new Yutong buses.

The Metrobus division are known as "camellos" (camels). The camellos operate the busiest routes and are trailers transformed into buses known as camels, so called for their two humps. It's a Cuban invention after the collapse of the Soviet Union in 1991 and the Special Period began. The Metrobus division purchased seven articulated buses which are currently serving the **M-5** camello line, covering a route from San Agustín in La Lisa municipality to Vedado. All camello trailers will be replaced by new articulated buses.

Public transportation MetroBus (former camello) routes:

- **M-1** *Alamar - Vedado* via Fraternidad
- **M-2** *Fraternidad - Santiago de Las Vegas*
- **M-3** *Alamar - Ciudad Deportiva*
- **M-4** *Fraternidad - San Agustin* via Marianao
- **M-5** *Vedado - San Agustin*
- **M-6** *Calvario - Vedado*
- **M-7** *Parque de la Fraternidad - Alberro* via Cotorro

Administration

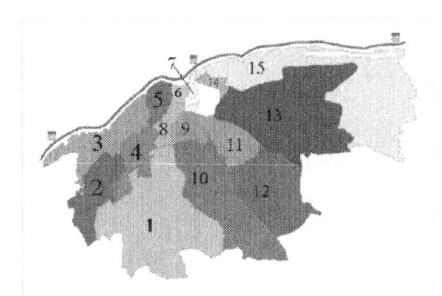

The 15 administrative divisions of Havana

Government

Havana is administered by a city council, with a mayor as chief administrative officer. The city is dependent upon the national government, however, for much of its budgetary and overall political direction. The national government is headquartered in Havana and plays an extremely visible role in the city's life. Moreover, the all-embracing authority of many national institutions, including the Communist Party of Cuba *(Partido Comunista de Cuba; PCC)*, the Revolutionary Armed Forces (Military of Cuba), the militia, and neighbourhood groups called the Committees for the Defense of the Revolution (CDRs), has led to a declining role for the city government, which, nevertheless, still provides such essential services as garbage collection and fire protection. The CDRs, which exist in virtually every street and apartment block, have two main functions: first, to actually defend the revolution against both external and internal opposition by keeping routine record of every resident's activities and, second, to handle routine tasks in maintaining neighborhoods.

José Martí Memorial, Plaza de la Revolución

Havana city borders are contiguous with the Habana Province. Thus Havana functions as both a city and a province. There are two joint councils upon which city and provincial authorities meet—one embraces municipal and provincial leaders on a national basis, the other, a Havana city and provincial council. Havana is divided into 15 constituent municipalities. Until 1976 there were six subdivisions, but in that year the city's borders were expanded to include the entire metropolitan area.

Municipios

The city is divided into 15 *municipios* - municipalities or boroughs. (Numbers refer to map above).

Municipality	Population (2004)	Area (km²)	Population Density (/km²)	Location	Remarks
Arroyo Naranjo	210053	83	2531	23°00′52″N 82°18′11″W	(10)
Boyeros	188593	134	1407	22°58′41″N 82°23′23″W	(1)
Centro Habana	158151	4	39538	23°08′9″N 82°22′56″W	(6)
Cerro	132351	10	13235	23°06′49″N 82°21′48″W	(8)
Cotorro	74650	66	1131	23°00′17″N 82°12′49″W	(12)
Diez de Octubre	227293	12	18941	23°05′49″N 82°20′24″W	(9)
Guanabacoa	112964	127	889	23°05′55″N 82°14′59″W	(13)
La Habana del Este	178041	145	1228	23°09′44″N 82°14′58″W	(15)
La Habana Vieja	95383	5	19077	23°08′14″N 82°21′57″W	(7)
La Lisa	131148	38	3451	23°01′57″N 82°28′42″W	(2)
Marianao	135551	21	6455	23°04′45″N 82°24′0″W	(4)
Playa	186959	36	5193	23°05′39″N 82°26′56″W	(3)
Plaza de la Revolución	161631	12	13469	23°08′0″N 82°23′15″W	(5)
Regla	44431	9	4937	23°08′11″N 82°18′5″W	(14)
San Miguel del Padrón	159273	26	6126	23°03′19″N 82°16′55″W	(11)

Source: Population from 2004 Census. Area from 1976 municipal re-distribution.

Demographics

Havana's rich cultural milieu included not only Spaniards from diverse regions of the Iberian Peninsula but other European peoples as well. In the era before Fidel Castro came to power, the city was economically and ethnically divided. On the one hand, there was the minority of the wealthy, educated elite, together with a strong middle class, and on the other was the working-class majority. This division was largely based on ethnic background: whites tended to be more well-to-do, while blacks and mulattoes generally were poor. The economic structure did not provide much opportunity for blacks and mulattoes except in the more menial occupations. There was also little opportunity for them to obtain an education. Under the Castro government that came to power in 1959, this system changed. Educational and employment opportunities were made available to Cubans of all ethnic backgrounds; however, top positions and fields of study were usually reserved only to signed communist party members and record showed supporters, though this has lost some strictness in recent years. In housing, the government follows an official policy of no discrimination based on ethnic background, and independent observers tend to believe this policy has been more or less faithfully carried out.

During the 18th, 19th and early part of the 20th century, large waves of Canarian, Catalan, and Galicians emigrated from the Iberian Peninsula to Havana.

- ﹏ Galician people
- ▮ Canarian people
- Catalan people

The Cuban government controls the movement of people into Havana on the grounds that the Havana metropolitan area (home to nearly 20% of the country's population) is overstretched in terms of land use, water, electricity, transportation, and other elements of the urban infrastructure. There is a population of internal migrants to Havana nicknamed "Palestinos" (Palestinians); these mostly hail from the eastern region of Oriente. Havana has a significant minority of Chinese, before the revolution the Chinese population counted to over 200,000, today Chinese born or ancestors could count up to 100,000. Havana also shelters a non-Cuban population of an unknown size, including Russians living mostly in Habana del Este that constantly emigrated during the Soviet era. There is a population of several thousand North African teen and pre-teen refugees.

Roman Catholics form the largest religious group in Havana. The Jewish community in Havana has reduced after the Revolution from once having embraced more than 15,000 Jews, many of whom had fled Nazi persecution and subsequently left Cuba to Miami or returned to Israel after Castro took to power in 1959. The city once had five synagogues, but only three remain (one Orthodox, one Conservative and one Sephardic). In February 2007 the New York Times estimated that there were about 1,500 known Jews living in Havana.

Infrastructure

Education

Further information: Education in Cuba

The national government assumes all responsibility for education, and there are adequate primary, secondary, and vocational training schools throughout Havana. The Cuban National Ballet School with 4,350 students is the biggest ballet school in the world and the most prestigious ballet school in Cuba, directed by *Ramona de Sáa*. In 2002 with the expansion of the school, out of 52,000 students interested to join the school, 4,050 were selected. All children receive an education. The schools are of varying quality and education is free and compulsory at all levels except higher learning, which is also free. The University of Havana, located in the Vedado section of Havana, was established in 1728 and was regarded as a leading institution of higher learning in the Western Hemisphere. Soon after the Revolution, the university, as well as all other educational institutions, were nationalized. Since then several other universities have opened, like the Polytechnic Institute "Joe Antonio Echeverria" where the vast majority of today's Cuban engineers are formed.

Health

Further information: Healthcare in Cuba

Under the Cuban government all citizens are covered by the national health care plan. Administration of the health care system for the nation is centred largely in Havana. Hospitals in Havana are run by the national government, and citizens are assigned hospitals and clinics to which they may go for attention. During the 1980s, Cuba began to attract worldwide attention for its treatment of heart diseases and eye problems, some of this treatment administered in Havana.[citation needed] There has long been now a high standard of health care in the city resulting from the Revolution.

Services

Utility services are under the control of several nationalized state enterprises that have developed since the Cuban revolution. Water, electricity, and sewage service are administered in this fashion. Electricity is supplied by generators that are fueled with oil. Much of the original power plant installations, which operated before the Revolutionary government assumed control, have become somewhat outdated. Electrical blackouts occurred, prompting the national government in 1986 to allocate the equivalent of $25,000,000 to modernize the electrical system. It is said that any part of Havana is within five minutes of a fire-fighting unit; the equipment is largely new.

Sports

Many Cubans are avid sports fans who particularly favour baseball. Havana's three baseball teams in the Cuban National Series are Industriales and Metropolitanos. The city has several large sports stadiums, the largest one is the Estadio Latinoamericano. Admission to sporting events is generally free, and impromptu games are played in neighborhoods throughout the city. Social clubs at the beaches provide facilities for water sports and include restaurants and dance halls.

- Havana was host to the 11th Pan American Games in 1991. Stadiums and facilities for this were built in the relatively unpopulated eastern suburbs.
- Havana was host to the 1992 IAAF World Cup in Athletics.
- Havana was a candidate to host the 2012 Summer Olympic Games, but was not shortlisted.

Notable people born in Havana

See also Category:People from Havana (category)

- Dave Lombardo, drummer (1965-)
- Roberto Goizueta, Coca-Cola Company CEO (1931–1997)
- Felipe Poey, zoologist (1799–1891)
- José Martí, poet, writer, nationalist leader (1853–1895)
- Ernesto Lecuona, composer, performer (1895–1963)
- Dulce María Loynaz, author (1902–1997)
- Alejo Carpentier, author (1904–1980)
- Daína Chaviano, author (1960-)
- José Lezama Lima, poet and author (1910–1976)
- Cundo Bermúdez, painter (1914–2008)
- Alicia Alonso, Prima Ballerina Assoluta (1920–)
- María Antonieta Pons, actress, Rumba dancer (1922–2004)
- Celia Cruz, singer (1925–2003)
- Elena Burke, singer (1928–2002)
- Alberto Korda, photographer, famous for his photo "Guerrillero Heróico" of Che Guevara (1928–2001)
- Camilo Cienfuegos, revolutionary along with Fidel Castro and Che Guevara (1932–1959)
- Ricardo Alarcón, politician, president of the National Assembly of Cuba (1937–)
- Felix Baloy, vocalist with the Afro Cuban All Stars and others (1943-)
- David Fumero, actor (1972–)
- Cristina Saralegui, journalist, talk show host (1948–)
- Oswaldo Payá, political activist (1952–)
- Alina Fernández, daughter and a critic of Fidel Castro (1956–)
- Andy García, actor (1956–)
- Elizabeth Caballero, International Opera Singer (1974–)
- Maria Teresa, Grand Duchess of Luxembourg, grand ducal consort of Grand Duke Henri of Luxembourg (1956–)
- Gloria Estefan, singer (1957–) (emigrated to the U.S. as a child)
- Carlos del Junco, musician (1958–)
- Al Jourgensen, musician (1958-)
- César Évora, actor (1959–)
- Juan Contino Aslán, politician, city mayor of Havana (1960-)
- Felipe Pérez Roque, politician, former foreign minister of Cuba (1965-)
- Humberto Padrón, film director (1967–)
- Pedro Álvarez Castelló, painter, (1967–2004)

- Rey Ruiz, musician (1970–)
- William Levy, actor (1979–)
- Yotuel Romero, musician (1976–)
- Michel Hernandez, MLB player for the Tampa Bay Rays, (1978-)
- Tony Fossas, MLB player for the Texas Rangers, Milwaukee Brewers, Boston Red Sox, St. Louis Cardinals, Seattle Mariners, Chicago Cubs, and the New York Yankees (1957-)
- George Lauzerique, MLB player for the Kansas City/Oakland Athletics and Milwaukee Brewers (1947-)
- Marcelino Lopez, MLB player for the Philadelphia Phillies, California Angels, Baltimore Orioles, Milwaukee Brewers, and the Cleveland Indians (1943-)
- Alex Sanchez, MLB player for the Milwaukee Brewers, Detroit Tigers, Tampa Bay Devil Rays, and the San Francisco Giants (1976-)
- Ivan Moffat, (1918–2002) screenwriter
- Dr. Alfonso Rodriguez Hidalgo, Minister/Theologian

Felipe Poey y Aloy
zoologist
(1799–1891)

José Martí
poet, writer, nationalist
leader
(1853–1895)

Ricardo Alarcón
politician
(1937–)

Andy García
actor
(1956–)

International relations

See also: List of twin towns and sister cities in the Caribbean

Twin towns — sister cities

Havana is twinned with:

- Barcelona, Spain
- Beijing, China
- Belgrade, Serbia
- Belo Horizonte, Brazil
- Bogotá, Colombia
- Caracas, Venezuela
- Cartagena, Colombia
- Constanţa, Romania
- Cuzco, Peru
- Esfahãn, Iran
- Glasgow, United Kingdom
- Istanbul, Turkey
- Madrid, Spain
- La Paz, Bolivia
- Manila, Philippines
- Mobile, United States
- Moscow, Russia
- Oaxaca, Mexico
- Porto Alegre, Brazil
- Rotterdam, Netherlands
- Saint Petersburg, Russia
- Salvador, Brazil
- Santiago, Dominican Republic
- Santo Domingo, Dominican Republic
- Santos, Brazil
- São Paulo, Brazil
- Seville, Spain
- Tehran, Iran
- Tijuana, Mexico
- Toledo, Spain
- Vitória, Brazil

See also

- Largest cities in the Americas

References

- King, Charles Spencer (2009) *Havana My Kind of Town*. USA: CreateSpace. ISBN 1-4404-3269-4.
- *Havana: History and Architecture of a Romantic City*. Alicia García Santana. Monacelli, October 2000. ISBN 1-58093-052-2.
- *The Rough Guide to Cuba* (3rd ed.). Rough Guides, May 2005. ISBN 1-84353-409-6.
- Barclay, Juliet (1993). *Havana: Portrait of a City*. London: Cassell. ISBN 1-84403-127-6 (2003 paperback edition). — A comprehensive account of the history of Havana from the early 16th century to the end of the 19th century.
- Carpentier, Alejo. *La ciudad de las columnas* (The city of columns). — A historical review of the city from one of the major authors in the iberoamerican literature, a native of this city.
- Cluster, Dick, & Rafael Hernández, *History of Havana.* New York: Palgrave-MacMillan, 2006. ISBN 1-4039-7107-2. A social history of the city from 1519 to the present, co-authored by a Cuban writer and editor resident in Havana and an American novelist and writer of popular history.
- Eguren, Gustavo. *La fidelísima Habana* (The very faithful Havana). — A fundamental illustrated book for those who wants to know the history of La Habana, includes chronicles, articles from natives and non natives, archives documents, and more.
- United Railways of Havana. Cuba: A Winter Paradise. 1908-1909, 1912–1913, 1914–1915 and 1915–1916 editions. New York, 1908, 1912, 1914 and 1915. Maps, photos and descriptions of

suburban and interurban electric lines.

- *Electric Traction in Cuba.* Tramway & Railway World (London), April 1, 1909, pp. 243–244. Map, photos and description of Havana Central Railroad.
- *The Havana Central Railroad.* Electrical World (New York), April 15, 1909, pp. 911–912. Text, 4 photos.
- *Three-Car Storage Battery Train.* Electric Railway Journal (New York), September 28, 1912, p. 501. Photo and description of Cuban battery cars.
- Berta Alfonso Gallol. Los Transportes Habaneros. Estudios Históricos. La Habana, 1991. The definitive survey (but no pictures or maps).
- *Six Days in Havana* by James A. Michener and John Kings. University of Texas Press; 1ST edition (1989). ISBN 978-0-292-77629-6. Interviews with close to 200 Cubans of widely assorted backgrounds and positions, and concerns how the country has progressed after 90 years of independence from Spain and under the 30-year leadership of Castro.
- One more interesting note about that edition of the New York Times: On page 5, there is a short blurb mentioning, "The plan for holding a Pan-American exhibition at Buffalo has been shelved for the present owing to the unsettled condition of the public mind consequent upon the Spanish-Cuban complications." President William McKinley was assassinated at the Pan-American Exhibition when it was finally held in 1901.
- "Havana Revisited: An Architectural Heritage" by Cathryn Griffith. W. W. Norton 2010. ISBN 978-0-393-73284-9 www.havanarevisited.com.

External links

- Havana travel guide from Wikitravel
- Havana, an external wiki [4]
- Havana from the Hotel Deauville [5]Photo Gallery
- www.lib.utexas.edu/maps [6], Central Havana Map
- contactcuba.com [7], Havana City Map
- havanatimes.org [8], Havana Travel Q & A
- Clickable map of Havana [9]
- "Fading Grandeur and Teeming Night Life Make Havana Hard to Resist" [10] by Victor Swoboda, *CanWest*, September 14, 2009
- "Searching for Cuba's Next Big Revolution" [11] by Spud Hilton, *San Francisco Chronicle*, April 19, 2009
- sophiaspring.com [12], Sophia Spring's Havana photographs from the series '50 Portraits of Cuba, 50 Years On'
- fotopedia.com [13], Selected photos of Havana
- Cuba: Hopeful in Havana [14] slideshow by *Life magazine*

- The Case of Havana, Cuba [15] by Mario Coyula and Jill Hamburg
- havanarevisited.com [16], "Havana Revisited: An Architectural Heritage" by Cathryn Griffith. W. W. Norton 2010
- Havana Club Rum: Cultural heritage

ace:Havana

Cityscape

Old Havana

Old Havana and its Fortifications*	
UNESCO World Heritage Site	
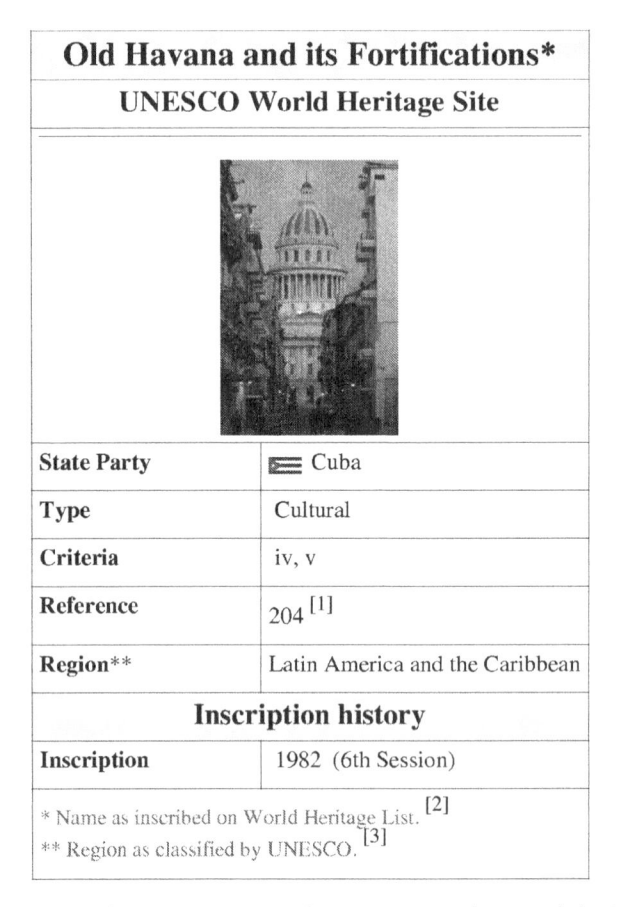	
State Party	▇ Cuba
Type	Cultural
Criteria	iv, v
Reference	204 [1]
Region**	Latin America and the Caribbean
Inscription history	
Inscription	1982 (6th Session)
* Name as inscribed on World Heritage List. [2] ** Region as classified by UNESCO. [3]	

Old Havana (Spanish: *La Habana Vieja*) contains the core of the original city of Havana. The positions of the original Havana city walls are the modern boundaries of Old Havana.

Old Havana is a UNESCO World Heritage Site and the name also refers to one of the municipalities of the city of Havana, Cuba, with the latter's boundaries extending to the south and west beyond the original city.

History

Havana Vieja was founded by the Spanish in 1519 in the natural harbor of the Bay of Havana. It became a stopping point for the treasure laden Spanish Galleons on the crossing between the New World and the Old World. In the 17th century it was one of the main shipbuilding centers. The city was built in baroque and neoclassic style. Many buildings have fallen in ruin in the later half of the 20th century, but a number are being restored. The narrow streets of old Havana contain many buildings, accounting for perhaps as many as one-third of the approximately 3,000 buildings found in Old Havana. It is the ancient city formed from the port, the official center and the Plaza de Armas. Old Havana was destroyed and burned by the French corsair Jacques de Sores. The pirate had taken Havana easily, plundering the city and burning much of it to the ground. After limiting the scarce defenders, De Sores left without obtaining the enormous wealth that he was hoping to find in Havana. The city remained devastated and set on fire. Since the incident, the Spanish brought soldiers and started building fortresses and walls to protect the city. Castillo de la Real Fuerza was the first fortress built; initiated in 1558, the construction was overseen by the engineer Bartolomé Sanchez.

Old Havana resembles Cadiz and Tenerife. Alejo Carpentier called it "de las columnas"(of the columns), but it could also be named for the gateways, the revoco, the deterioration and the rescue, the intimacy, the shade, the cool, the courtyards... In her there are all the big ancient monuments, the forts, the convents and churches, the palaces, the alleys, the arcade, the human density. The Cuban State has undertaken enormous efforts to preserve and to restore Old Havana through the efforts of the Office of the Historian of the City, directed by Eusebio Leal.

Main sights

- The Malecón is the avenue that runs along the seawall at the northern shore of Havana, from Habana Vieja to the Almendares River.
- Castillo del Morro, picturesque fortress guarding the entrance to Havana bay. The construction of the castle Los Tres Reyes del Morro owed to the step along in Havana of the English pirate Sir Francis Drake. The king of Spain arranged its construction on a big stone which was known by the name of El Morro. He sent the field master Juan de Texeda, accompanied of the military engineer Battista Antonelli, who came to Havana in 1587 and began the task at once.
- La Cabaña fortress, located on the east side of the Havana Bay. The most impressive fortress of the Spanish colony was La Cabaña. It impresses with its 18th century walls, constructed at the same time as El Morro. Every night at 9 p.m., some soldiers dressed in suits of the epoch shoot from her the "el cañonazo de las nueve", (gunshot of the nine). It went off every day to warn of the closing of the doors of the wall that surrounded the city.
- San Salvador de la Punta Fortress, In the shore opposite to the Castle of El Morro, at the beginning of the curve of El Malecon, there rises the fortress of San Salvador de la Punta, of minor architectural dimensions. It was constructed in 1590, and in 1629 the Chapter of Havana decided, to

defend better the port, to join her in the night with the El Morro by using a thick chain that prevented the entry of enemy ships.

- Castillo de la Real Fuerza, The fortress or (lit.) Castle of the Royal Army is another big monument that closes the Plaza de las Armas. It was the first big fortification of the city, initiated in 1558 on the ruins of an ancient fortress. In the same year, the Crown sent to Cuba the engineer Bartolomé Sanchez, supervised by 14 official and main stonemasons in order to reconstruct the castle, which had been set fire and destroyed by the French corsair Jacques de Sores.
- Catedral de San Cristóbal, the most prominent building on the *Plaza de la Catedral*. The Cathedral was raised on the chapel after 1748 by order of the bishop from Salamanca, Jose Felipe de Trespalacios. It is one of the most beautiful and sober churches of the American baroque.
- National Capitol, styled after the Panthéon (Paris), looking similar to the U.S. Capitol.
- Galician Center, Central Park, The Galician Center, of neobarroque style was establish as a social club of the Galician emigrants between 1907 and 1914. Built on the Theater Tacon (nowadays Great Theater of Havana), it was open during the Carnival of 1838 with five masked dances.
- Plaza de Armas - the main touristic square. The origin of its name is military, since from the end of the 16th century the ceremonies and the military events took place here.
- Gran Teatro de la Habana, the Great Theater of Havana is famous, particularly for the acclaimed National Ballet of Cuba and its founder Alicia Alonso. It sometimes performs the National Opera. The theater is also known as concert hall, Garcia Lorca, the biggest in Cuba.
- The Museum of the Revolution, located in the former Presidential Palace, with the boat Granma on display in front of the museum.
- San Francisco de la Habana Basilica, Habana Vieja, The set of church and convent of San Francisco de Asis, byline of the year 1608, and it was reconstructed in 1737.

Threats to Old Havana

In 2008, Hurricane Ike destroyed many structures in Old Havana, overturning years of conservation work directed at the iconic antiquated buildings of the area. Not only did it damage historic buildings, but it forced many of Old Havana's residents to flee for safety. The threats that hurricanes pose adds to an already tenuous state for Old Havanas many historic buildings. Age, decay, and neglect combine with natural factors in a complex set of threats to the long-term preservation of this historic old town.

UNESCO Heritage site

In 1982, La Habana Vieja was inscribed in the UNESCO World Heritage List. A safeguarding campaign was launched a year later to restore the authentic character of the buildings.

Photo gallery

El Morro Castle

San Cristóbal Cathedral

Great Theater of Havana

Plaza de la Catedral a La Habana

Twinnings

* Torrelavega, Spain
* Viveiro, Spain
* Cartagena, Colombia
* Guanajuato, Guanajuato, Mexico
* Sintra, Portugal, since 2000

See also

- World Heritage Site
- Havana

External links

- Links to sites with casa particular and travel info on Old Havana [4]

References

Geographical coordinates: 23°08′09.4″N 82°21′30.0″W

Arroyo Naranjo, Cuba

Arroyo Naranjo	
— Municipality —	
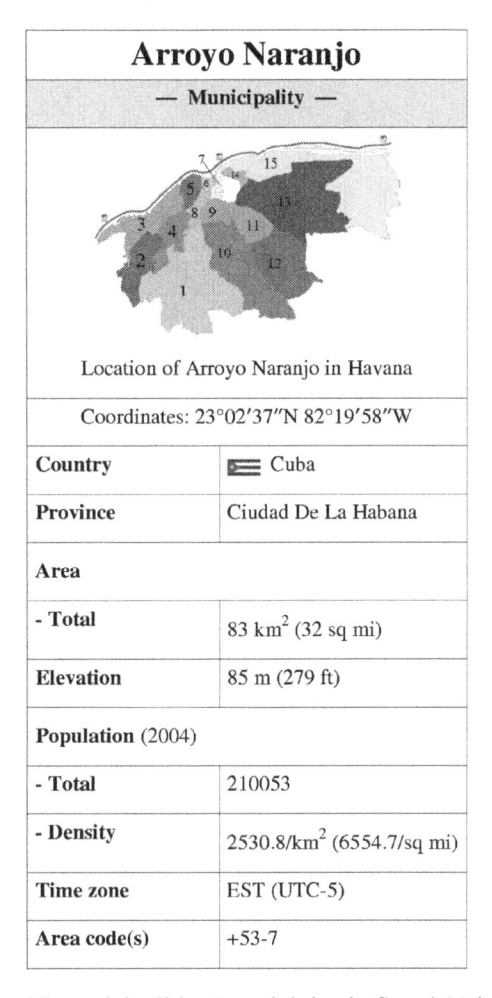 Location of Arroyo Naranjo in Havana	
Coordinates: 23°02′37″N 82°19′58″W	
Country	Cuba
Province	Ciudad De La Habana
Area	
- **Total**	83 km^2 (32 sq mi)
Elevation	85 m (279 ft)
Population (2004)	
- **Total**	210053
- **Density**	2530.8/km^2 (6554.7/sq mi)
Time zone	EST (UTC-5)
Area code(s)	+53-7

Arroyo Naranjo is one of the 15 municipalities (municipios in Spanish) in the city of Havana, Cuba. It became part of Havana city while the capital grew.

History

The borough was founded in 1845, and by 1848 its party was created. Arroyo Naranjo is situated 11 kilometers (7 mi) south of Old Havana on the Havana-Las Vegas highway, having been a stop of buses that were doing the service between these two cities. In 1858 Arroyo Naranjo had 291 inhabitants, who were increasing in the period of the baths, for the proximity to the medicinal waters known by the *Cacahual*. Arroyo Naranjo had always a progressive population. From 291 inhabitants of 1858, in 1871 the town had 1,485.

Demographics

In 2004, the municipality of Arroyo Naranjo had a population of 210,053. With a total area of 83 km^2 (32.0 sq mi), it has a population density of 2530.8 /km^2 (6554.7/sq mi).

See also

- Municipalities of Cuba
- List of cities in Cuba

Boyeros

Boyeros
— Municipality —
Welcome sign in Boyeros near airport
Location of Boyeros in Havana
Coordinates: 23°00′26″N 82°24′6″W

Country	🏳 Cuba
Province	Ciudad De La Habana
Established	1976 (Municipality)
Area	
- Total	134 km^2 (51.7 sq mi)
Elevation	65 m (213 ft)
Population (2004)	
- Total	188593
- Density	1407.4/km^2 (3645.1/sq mi)
Time zone	EST (UTC-5)
Area code(s)	+53-7

Boyeros is one of the 15 municipalities or boroughs (*municipios* in Spanish) in the city of Havana, Cuba.

The municipality was created in 1976, and amalgamated the town of Santiago de Las Vegas. It lies on the south-west side of the city and extends towards the José Martí International Airport.

Demographics

In 2004, the municipality of Boyeros had a population of 188,593. With a total area of 134 km^2 (51.7 sq mi), it has a population density of 1407.4 /km^2 (3645.1/sq mi).

It is divided into seven *consejos populares* (wards)- Santiago de Las Vegas, Nuevo Santiago, Boyeros, Wajay, Calabazar, Altahabana and Armada.

History

During the 18th, 19th and early part of the 20th century, large waves of Canarian people emigrated to Boyeros.

See also

- Municipalities of Cuba
- List of cities in Cuba

Santiago de Las Vegas

Santiago de Las Vegas (Santiago de Compostela de las Vegas)	
Location of Santiago de las Vegas in Cuba	
Coordinates: 22°58′39″N 82°22′41″W	
Country	🏳 Cuba
Province	La Habana
Founded	1683
Established	1725 (town)
	1824 (city)
Elevation	90 m (295 ft)
Population (2000)	
- Total	22000
Time zone	EST (UTC-5)
Area code(s)	+53-7

Santiago de las Vegas is a city in Havana Province, Cuba, located 12 miles (19 km) south of Havana. As of the year 2000, the population was 22,000. The Cuban government maintains an agricultural experiment station, as well as a meteorology center in the city.

History

The first settlement dates from 1683 when tobacco farmers settled on the lands of the ranches in Sócalo Hondo, Managua, Bejucal and La Chorrera, then under the jurisdiction of the Roman Catholic Archdiocese of Santiago de Compostela. The population grew quickly and in 1694 the first church was built. On June 18, 1725, the settlement was incorporated as the town of *Santiago de Compostela de las Vegas* by royal certificate and was granted an extensive jurisdictional demarcation to the town. This marked the growth of its political and economic importance.

In 1824, the town was declared a city, allowing their people to raise a statue dedicated to the Spanish King Ferdinand VII, placed at the Recreo Square. In 1831, the monarch corresponded by granting the city with the title of Faithful and Very Illustrious City Council.

In 1836, a government land ownership was created for the city, but in 1840 was instead awarded to Bejucal; however, it was returned again to Santiago de las Vegas in 1845. The city's church was completed in 1800; one of its towers was destroyed by a hurricane in 1846. The cemetery was built in 1814 and closed in 1895 to use the new one built at that times. In 1911 the *Consistorial House* was built.

The population grew from 3300 in 1861 to almost 11,000 in 1953.

Santiago de las Vegas lost its municipality status in 1976 under the new Political-Administrative Division created by the government of Fidel Castro, and is now part of the new municipality of Boyeros, thus being amalgamated into the City of Havana.

Commerce and business

Transportation is one of the primary industries for the city. Geographically located between the increasingly greater metropolitan zones of the island and the rural region to the south and southwest of the province of Havana, it served as a distribution point of numerous passengers between these two regions. Its bus station was a title branch of the National Bus Station in Havana.

Here was born, in 1923, the Italian writer Italo Calvino. It was also the birthplace of the notorious scientist Juan Tomás Roig Mesa, renowned botanist well-known by his work on medicinal and poisonous plants. Other notable sons of the city were ethnomusicologist Helio Orovio and mezzo-soprano Esther Borja.

In addition, Santiago de las Vegas has three of the most important sanatoriums of Cuba, the Psychiatric Hospital of Mazorra, the "Los Cocos" sanatorium for housing and caring of HIV/AIDS patients, and the Sanatorium of El Rincón for leprosy patients. The presence of these facilities has also increased the necessity of lodging and restaurants in the community.

Tourism

The construction of the José Martí International Airport in Havana brought important opportunities for the development of the tourist industry. Santiago de las Vegas has natural, historical, cultural and religious points of interest. These opportunities have created another possible source of wealth for the city and its surroundings, leading to the construction of hotels, restaurants, and other facilities, as well as created new jobs.

The most massive religious celebration in Cuba is the festivity of San Lázaro, on December 17. On the days before, tens of thousands of devouts, revelers, tourists and curious gather in pilgrimage to the shrine of El Rincón, some of them dressed in sackcloth or purple clothing and carrying bizarre penances to pay gratitude to the miraculous San Lázaro, identified with the yoruba deity of Babalu Aye.

External links

- Santiago de las Vegas: an illustrated history of a Cuban town, 1882-1959. [1]
- Virtual Home of Santiago de las Vegas (Blog). [2]

Geographical coordinates: 22°58′40″N 82°22′40″W

Centro Habana

<table>
<tr><td colspan="2" align="center">Centro Habana
— Municipality —</td></tr>
<tr><td colspan="2">
Centro Havana seen from Hotel Habana Libre</td></tr>
<tr><td colspan="2">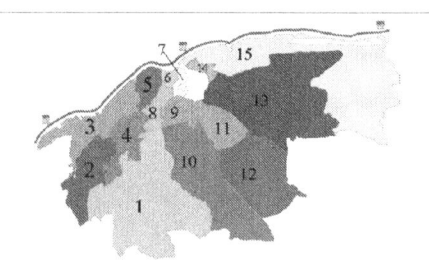
Location of Centro Habana in Havana</td></tr>
<tr><td colspan="2" align="center">Coordinates: 23°08′0″N 82°23′0″W</td></tr>
<tr><td>Country</td><td>Cuba</td></tr>
<tr><td>Province</td><td>Ciudad De La Habana</td></tr>
<tr><td>Area</td><td></td></tr>
<tr><td>- Total</td><td>4 km^2 (1.5 sq mi)</td></tr>
<tr><td>Elevation</td><td>45 m (148 ft)</td></tr>
<tr><td>Population (2004)</td><td></td></tr>
<tr><td>- Total</td><td>158151</td></tr>
<tr><td>- Density</td><td>39537.8/km^2 (102402.4/sq mi)</td></tr>
<tr><td>Time zone</td><td>EST (UTC-5)</td></tr>
<tr><td>Area code(s)</td><td>+53-7</td></tr>
</table>

Centro Habana is one of the 15 municipalities (municipios in Spanish) in the city of Havana, Cuba. There are a lot of retail spaces (such as *Plaza de Carlos III* commercial center, office buildings, hotels, bars and clubs (such as the *Casa de la Musica* on Galliano). A chinatown - *Barrio Chino* - is also located in this district. It is a smaller municipality of Havana, and it has the highest population density.

The infrastructure of the city, built 450 years ago, heavily deteriorated during the 1990s after the collapse of the Cuban-Soviet trade partnership. In 1996, restoration projects were started to improve housing and infrastructure in the Cayo Hueso community.

Demographics

In 2004, the municipality of Centro Habana had a population of 158,151. With a total area of 4 km^2 (1.5 sq mi), it has a population density of 39537.8 /km^2 (102402.4/sq mi).

External links

- Centro Habana guia turistica [1] - touristic guide (Spanish)

Cerro, Cuba

Cerro is one of the 15 municipalities (municipios in Spanish) in the city of Havana, Cuba. The area dates from 1803 when two property owners, *José Maria Rodríguez* and *Francisco Betancourt*, established residence. Their example was followed by many others. In 1807, Cerro was recognized as a town, with the construction of the first wooden church, which has been replaced by the current parish buildings.

Cerro was chosen the wealthy families of the capital as a place to spend the summer. In 1843 there existed five large vacation residences, with 23 others notable for their sumptuousness. There were also 273 private homes owned by wealthy families. In 1843, Cerro's population was 2,125 inhabitants and by 1858, 2,530 permanent residents.

Geographical coordinates: 23°06′49″N 82°21′48″W

Cotorro, Cuba

Cotorro, or *San Pedro del Cotorro*, is one of the 15 municipalities (*municipios* in Spanish) in the city of Havana, Cuba. The municipality is situated by the Central Highway (Carretera Central), and main *autopista* (motorway). By the end of the 50s, Cotorro had grown in such a way that it was exceeding in extension and population to the head of the municipality. Cotorro is 16 km from Old Havana. Its foundation dates to 1822.

El Cotorro cuenta con varias zonas como son: Loteria, Centro del Cotorro, Las Brisas, El Berro y Nuevo Cotorro. Se extiende desde los limites de San Francisco de Paula al Oeste hasta la entrada de San Jose De las Lajas al Este al Norte le queda Santa Maria del Rosario y al Sur le queda el municipio Arroyo Naranjo . Este Municipio tiene este nombre ya que en el siglo 18 o 19 el Restaurante, Motel "El Oasis" unos de los restaurantes mas famosos de esa epoca ya que servia de parada a todo viajero que iba de pasada tenia un dueno que muchos dicen que tenia una nariz como la de un cotorro y desde ese momento todos empezaron a llamarle El Cotorro.

Tiene tambien varias industrias una de las industrias mas grandes de Cuba la Empresa Siderurgica Antilla De Acero esta industria abarca una extension bastante larga que va desde calle 20 hasta calle 100. Fue creada desde los anos 50 y tubo un desarrollo grande es la epoca de los 80 gracias a la ayuda de la antigua Union Sovietica. Tambien tiene la Cervezeria Hatuey en los anos antes 1959 los duenos de la Hatuey ya tenia una Cervezeria en el Oriente en Cuba y deciden abrir otra Cervezeria la cual tambien haria Malta con el mismo nombre esta Cerveza es muy famosa para los cubanos ya que fue una de las unicas Cervezas en hacerce con un grado en alcohol bastante alto en los anos 80 ya tenia una Hatuey de 18 grados de Alcohol y luego sale otra con 24 grados en Alcohol no se vendio mucho ya que con una cerveza o dos se veia el efecto.

Tiene tambien varias escuelas como son Quitin Banderas, Vitalio Acuna, Gervasio Cabrera, 9 De Abril, Juan Gualberto Gomez, Pedro Luis Ferrer, Los Camilitos, Martires De Barbados entre otras esta ultima es una escuela solamente de desportes.

External links

- Site Web Cotorro [1]
- Site Web of Culture Cotorro [2]

Diez de Octubre, Cuba

Diez de Octubre is one of the 15 municipalities (*municipios* in Spanish) in the city of Havana, Cuba. It is one of the oldest municipalities of the capital. Its foundation dates from the second half of the 17th Century aimed at populating the city when the Canary Islanders emigrate to Cuba.

Geographical coordinates: 23°05'17"N 82°21'35"W

Guanabacoa

Guanabacoa is a colonial township in eastern Havana, Cuba, and one of the 15 municipalities of the city. It is famous for its historical Santería and is home to the first African Cabildo in Havana. It was the site of the Battle of Guanabacoa, a skirmish between British and Spanish troops during the Battle of Havana during the Seven Years' War.

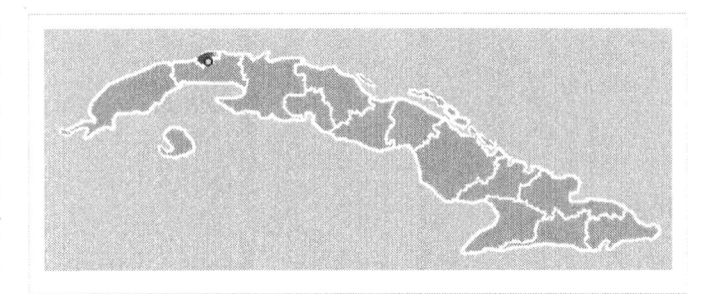

Trivia

- Four Major League Baseball players were born in Guanabacoa: Emilio Palmero (1895), Tony Ordenana (1918), Rene Valdez (1929), and Evelio Hernández (1931). Also news reporter Rick Sanchez (1958) was born in Guanabacoa.
- The fictional Peña family featured in the PBS comedy series ¿Qué Pasa, USA? were natives of Guanabacoa.

External links

- Guanabacoa [1] in Ciudades, Pueblos y Lugares Cubanos/Guije.com. (In Spanish.) Website about the town's history prior to 1960. The pictures in this site have all been taken after 1960. The viewer will see significant decay thoroughout the pictures, whereas Guanabacoa was a prosperous town before the Castro regime took over, neglect, apathy and poverty have turned this once properous town with beautiful colonial architecture into a mass of dilapidated buildings.

Geographical coordinates: 23°07'N 82°18'W

Habana del Este

Habana del Este (Spanish for "Havana of the East" or Eastern Havana) is one of the municipalities forming the city of Havana. As its name indicates it is on the eastern side of the city, and includes the overspill towns of Camilo Cienfuegos and Alamar as well as the beach towns of Boca Ciega, Tarara, Santa María del Mar and Guanabo.

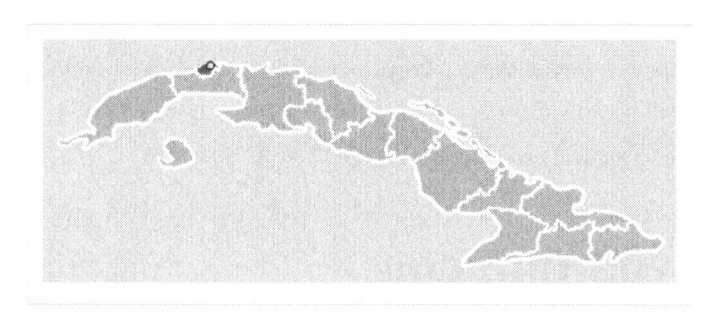

Beaches snapshots

Beaches

The chain of beaches called the Eastern Beaches (Spanish: *Playas del Este*) extend for 15 miles along the north coast of Havana City province.

The Eastern Beaches are (named from West to East): Tarará; El Mégano; Bacuranao (has a bay shape, thick sand and a small spanish fortress on its western side); Santa María del Mar; Boca Ciega; Guanabo; La Veneciana and Brisas del Mar. The Eastern Beaches are a very popular tourist spot with excellent natural conditions, though their facilities are very scarce and yet to be expanded.

External links

- details of municipality [1] (Spanish)

Geographical coordinates: 23°09′33.0″N 82°16′15.8″W

La Lisa, Cuba

La Lisa is one of the 15 municipalities (*municipios* in Spanish) in the city of Havana, Cuba.

It has several neighbourhoods such as Alturas de la Lisa, El Cano, Punta Brava.etc

It can be generally thought of as a semi-rural municipality.

Geographical coordinates: 23°01′29″N 82°27′47″W

Marianao

Marianao is a town and municipality in the province of the city of Havana, Cuba, 6 miles southwest of the original city of Havana, with which it is connected by the Marianao railway. As of 1989, the municipality had a population of 133,016. Marianao is on a range of hills about 1500 ft. above sea level, is noted for its salubrious climate. The city dates from about 1830.

As the Havana expanded during the 1930s and 1940s, Marianao became a suburb of the city.

A famous landmark is the monument built to honor Carlos J. Finlay. Mr. Finlay was a doctor who helped eradicate yellow fever in Cuba in the 19th century. What is interesting about this building is the fact that it is shaped like a syringe. The monument is at the junction of *calles* 100 y 31, close to several major hospitals.

Marianao is home to the famous Tropicana Club and was home to the Oriental Park Racetrack.

Famous people from Marianao

Moved off the island

- Luis Tiant, Baseball Player
- Maria Teresa, Grand Duchess of Luxembourg, spouse of the current Grand Duke of Luxembourg
- Camilo Marin, Jockey Agent

External links

- details of municipality [1] (Spanish)

References

- ⓦ This article incorporates text from a publication now in the public domain: Chisholm, Hugh, ed (1911). *Encyclopædia Britannica* (Eleventh ed.). Cambridge University Press.

Geographical coordinates: 23°05′N 82°26′W

The most complete description of the City of Marianao before the 1959 Revolution

- http://www.lenzayas.com/Marianao/Marianao.htm

Playa, Havana

Playa is one of the 15 municipalities of the City of Havana, Cuba. It is the most north-western of them. It stretches from the Almendares River in the east, to Santa Fe in the west. On the north is the sea. The word "playa" means "beach" in Spanish.

It includes the upmarket district of Miramar and the former fishing village of Jaimanitas. Other districts include Flores, Nautico, Siboney, Kohly and Buena Vista - home of the original Buena Vista Social Club.

External links

- Cubasi [1] - Details of municipality (Spanish)

Geographical coordinates: 23°05′39″N 82°26′56″W

Miramar, Havana

Miramar, Ciudad de La Habana is an upscale district in the municipality of Playa in the city of Havana.

Many embassies, including the landmark Russian embassy, are located in Miramar - in particular on *Quinta Avenida* (Fifth Avenue).

This is a beautiful residential area (one of the better parts of Havana). Before the Revolution, this was an upscale neighbourhood. There are many large houses and mansions here. This district and the Country Club (Siboney) were the most glamorous spaces in the Havana of the 50s. There are also some of Havana's more modern hotels such as Hotel Melia Habana, Oasis Panorama Hotel and Occidental Miramar, beaches and private rental houses (*known as casas particulares*). Also located here is the International School of Havana.

In the late 1990s and 2000s, the have been built several office blocks in a complex called *Centro de Negocios Miramar* - the "Miramar Trade Center".

The church "Jesus de Miramar" on Quinta Avenida in Miramar.

The landmark Russian embassy in Miramar.

Teatro Miramar

Built in the 1950s, the 600-seat theatre was still in use as a cultural centre for the local community until around 18 years ago, but the collapse of the Soviet Union as one of Cuba's main trading partners, coupled with the US economic blockade made it impossible to obtain the equipment needed for essential repair work to the theatre. The Miramar theatre lies at the heart of the Playa district of Havana. Originally built as a grand theatre, over time the building was used as a cinema and meeting place for local people. Like most buildings in Cuba it has been battered by hurricanes and degraded by humidity. But due to a chronic shortage of funds the theatre never received the regular maintenance required in that climate, and fell into decay.

A Grand Renovation for Teatro Miramar

Teatro Miramar sat neglected and exposed to hurricanes and humidity for many years, with little to attention being paid to the once grand play-house in Havana's Playa district. Built in the 1950s when Cuba, and especially Havana, were glittering with pomp and wealth, Teatro Miramar was a grand and regal venue for 18 years. It was the fall of the U.S.S.R. coupled with the trading embargoes of the U.S.A. which halted any economic relief or much needed equipment to maintain the 600 seat Teatro Miramar.

To recreate Miramar into the grand shrine of local and international talent it once was will not be an easy task, as the years of relentless humidity, hurricanes, termites, and other natural factors have taken their toll on Teatro Miramar.

Proposed for restoration by Centro Nacional de Escuales de Arte (CNEArt) 2006 as one of the nation's most important projects for education and art. Restoration and renovation is planned for the enlarging of the stage, improving the lights, and adding a video screen. Renovation to the exterior of the building is also set to begin. Once complete, the stage area will be large enough for a circus to perform. Organizers also hope that Teatro Miramar will be used for international festivals.

Teatro Director Juvenal Garcia Beato is using the space for an arts school, with 80 - 100 local children graduating each year. A visit to Teatro Miramar may find a dance troupe of pre-teen girls practicing for an up-coming show, each girl wearing ballet shoes donated by the Birmingham and Royal Ballet.

To avoid disruption to the school and its students, an adjoining building was renovated and is being used while grand renovations to Teatro Miramar are underway. Upon completion, the adjoining building will be a dedicated practice area, giving more room to the teatro for performances, classes.

Geographical coordinates: 23°7′21″N 82°25′10″W

Plaza de la Revolución

Plaza de la Revolución Revolution Square
— Municipality —

Plaza of the Revolution and the Ministry of the Interior seen from the José Martí memorial
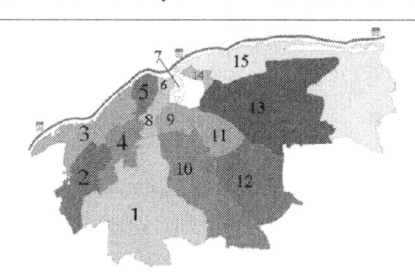
Location of Plaza de la Revolución in Havana
Coordinates: 23°07′28″N 82°23′10″W

Country	▨ Cuba
Province	Ciudad De La Habana
Area	
- Total	12 km^2 (4.6 sq mi)
Elevation	30 m (98 ft)
Population (2004)	
- Total	161631
- Density	13469.3/km^2 (34885.3/sq mi)
Time zone	EST (UTC-5)

Area code(s)	+53-7

Plaza de la Revolución ("Revolution Square") is a municipality and a square in Havana, Cuba.

The municipality stretches from the square down to the sea at the Malecón and includes the Vedado district.

Square

Revolution Square and the José Martí Memorial

The Plaza is one of the world's largest city squares, measuring 72000 square meters.

The square is notable as being where many political rallies take place and Fidel Castro and other political figures address Cubans. Fidel Castro has addressed more than a million Cubans on many important occasions, such as 1 May and 26 July each year.

The square is dominated by the José Martí Memorial, which features a 109 m (358 ft) tall tower and an 18 m (59 ft) statue. The National Library, many government ministries, and other buildings are located in and around the Plaza. Located behind the memorial are the closely guarded offices of former President Fidel Castro. Opposite the memorial on the far side of the square is the famous Che Guevara image with the slogan 'Hasta la Victoria Siempre' (Forever Onwards Towards Victory) that identifies the Ministry of the Interior building.

Construction of the square and the José Martí monument commenced during the Presidency of Fulgencio Batista. The square and the memorial were completed in 1959 (the year Fidel Castro came to power). It was originally called Plaza Cívica (Civic Square). After the Cuban Revolution (1959), it was renamed "Plaza de la Revolución" or "Revolution Square." An elevator allows access the top of the memorial, at 109 m one the tallest points in the city.

Demographics

In 2004, the municipality of Plaza de la Revolución had a population of 161,631. With a total area of 12 km^2 (4.6 sq mi), it has a population density of 13469.3 /km^2 (34885.3/sq mi).

Landmarks in Plaza

Iconic Ministry of Interior Defense Building in Plaza.

Comité Central del Partido Comunista de Cuba Building. (Communist Party headquarters)

Memorial Jose Marti Monumental statue and lookout, at 109 m it is one of the tallest points in the city.

Teatro Nacional de Cuba. (National Theater of Cuba)

Ministry of Interior building in Plaza de la Revolución (Revolution Square) taken on January 24, 2008

See also

- Municipalities of Cuba
- List of cities in Cuba

External links

- "Historia del memorial" [1] (in Spanish). Memorial José Martí. Archived from the original [2] on 3 February 2007. Retrieved 26 March 2007.
- Havana's Che Guevara Mural gets a Twin [3] by the Moon Travel Guide

Vedado

Vedado (Spanish: *El Vedado*) is the downtown and a vibrant neighbourhood in the city of Havana, Cuba. Bordered on the east by Central Havana, and on the west by the Miramar/Playa district. The main street running east to west is Calle 23, also known as 'La Rampa'. The northern edge of the district is the waterfront breakwater known as the Malecón, a famous and popular place for social gatherings in the city. The United States Interests Section complex is located in Vedado. Vedado is part of the municipality Plaza de la Revolucion.

Geography

Notable sites

Among the notable sites in Vedado are the Gran Sinagoga Bet Shalom and the Centro Hebreo Sefaradi de Cuba. Many of the hotels are also located in Vedado, like the Melia Cohiba Hotel and Hotel Riviera.

Also in Vedado is the park known as John Lennon Park, for the statue of Lennon that is there.

Hotel Nacional, open since 1930

Nearby neighborhoods include:

- To the east: Central Havana
- To the west: Miramar

Geographical coordinates: 23°07′52″N 82°23′39″W

Regla

Regla is one of the 15 municipalities of Havana, Cuba. It comprises the town of Regla, located at the bottom of Havana Bay in a former aborigine settlement named Guaicanamar, in a peninsula dividing Marimelena from Guasabacoa inlets and the village of Casablanca, located and the entry of the Havana Bay.

The town is a commercial and industrial suburb with shipyards: Galainela shipyard, ENA drydock, till recently operated as a joint venture with Curacao CDM and the Navy's shipyard at Casablanca, docks,including the TCH (Havana Container Terminal), the Ñico Lopez refinery, formerly Shell Refinary and popularly known as Belot Refinery due to the location, the Fluor and Wheat Mills and the aviation fuel depots.

It is known for its rich colonial history, being the home town of Chacón, Guaracheros de Regla and the traditional Virgen de Regla Santería celebrations. It formed during the colonial period around the hermitage of Nuestra Senora de Regla (est. 1690) and was officially founded in 1687 (1765).

Regla has a strong patriotic tradition being home to several patriots and personalities, among others Eduardo Facciolo, executed by the colonial Spanish government for conspiring for Cuban independence and Eduardo Coyula, who reached the rank of Leutenant Colonel of the Cuban Liberation Army (Mambi Army) fighting against colonial Spain.

It is an historic known fact that the first speech with political pro-independentist overtunes delivered by National Apostle José Martí was delivered in the Liceum of Regla.

During the struggle against dictator Fulgencio Batista, the town was described as "sierra chiquita" little mountain range in alussion to the rebels in the Sierra Maestra range due to the strong opposition to Batista.

Demographics

In 2004, the municipality of Regla had a population of 44,431. With a total area of 9 km^2 (3.5 sq mi), it has a population density of 4936.8 /km^2 (12786.3/sq mi).

Regla is divided into Barrios or Colonias, including Reparto Modelo, La Colonia, La Loma and La Colina Lenin.

Regla is divided into three Consejos Populares (People's Council) the grassroot local government form in Cuba namely Guaicanamar, comprising Regla downtown, Loma-Modelo, comprising Regla suburbs and Casablanca, comprising the village of same name and surrounds.

Twin towns

- ▮ ▮ Corsico, Italy, since 2003
- ▀▀▀ Richmond, USA

See also

- Municipalities of Cuba
- List of cities in Cuba
- Jose Canseco

External links

- Unofficial Regla Sister City Web Site [1]

Geographical coordinates: 23°07′54″N 82°20′11″W

Does not have the meaning of the spanish word regla

San Miguel del Padrón

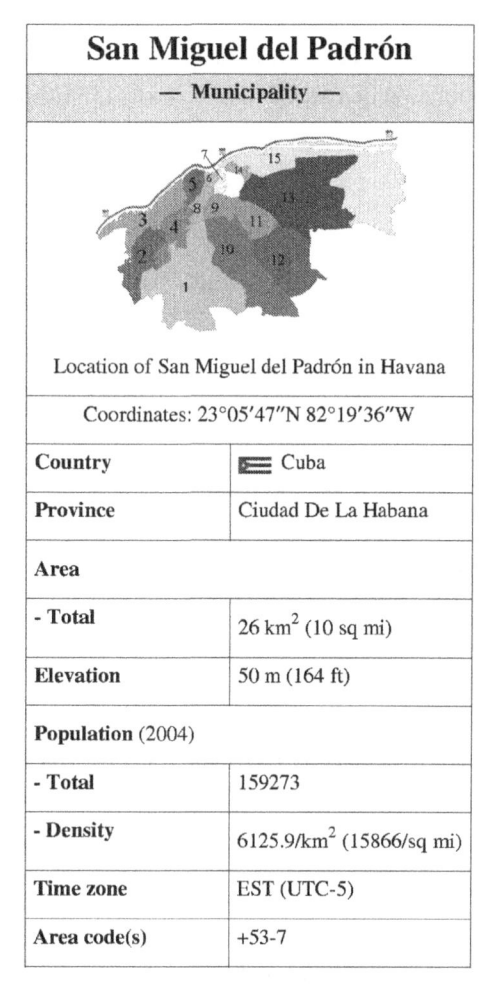

San Miguel del Padrón

— Municipality —

Location of San Miguel del Padrón in Havana

Coordinates: 23°05′47″N 82°19′36″W

Country	Cuba
Province	Ciudad De La Habana
Area	
- Total	26 km^2 (10 sq mi)
Elevation	50 m (164 ft)
Population (2004)	
- Total	159273
- Density	6125.9/km^2 (15866/sq mi)
Time zone	EST (UTC-5)
Area code(s)	+53-7

San Miguel del Padrón is a municipality in Havana city, Cuba. It is one of the 15 municipalities into which the city is divided. It is on Havana's south-eastern outskirts, stretching from Ciudad Mar to Diezmero and from Reparto Mañana to Caballo Blanco.

This vast demographic area was unpopulated in the late 40s, with small pockets of wealthy and land owners. It became heavily populated during the early 60s with the emergence of Corea (name given to a stretch of terrain clandestinely occupied by the homeless after being evicted from the main city areas) and new houses along the main street (Calzada de San Miguel). By the mid 60s the town became administratively adjacent to Guanabacoa.

San Miguel has been notorious for musicians, professional dancers and afro Cuban religious practitioners (Santeria, Lukumi, Palo). During the early 70s it was judicially declared one of the most troublesome towns in Havana due to a high degree of black market goods and comestibles.

Demographics

In 2004, the municipality of San Miguel del Padrón had a population of 159,273. With a total area of 26 km^2 (10.0 sq mi), it has a population density of 6125.9 /km^2 (15866/sq mi).

See also

- Municipalities of Cuba
- List of cities in Cuba

Guanabo

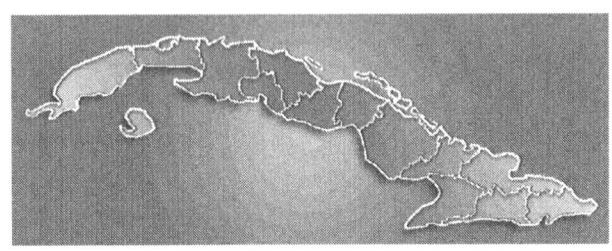

Location of Guanabo in Cuba

Guanabo is a town in the Ciudad de la Habana Province of Cuba. It is located within the municipality of Habana del Este halfway between the centre of Havana and Santa Cruz del Norte, at the mouth of the *Guanabo River*, between the Atlantic Ocean coast and the *Sierra del Canchón* (mountain range).

Guanabo is a seaside touristic town, with small scale villas and a few low rise hotels.

The town was founded in 1800. In 1827 it was the place where the *Peñas Altas* uprising was crushed by troops from Havana (Peñas Altas is a neighbourhood east of Guanabo).

In the late 1990s it was known as a sexual tourism destination.Wikipedia:Avoid weasel words Prostitution has since been cracked down by large police interventions, and (as of 2005) it is not uncommon to see police units constantly patrolling the town.[citation needed]

Overview of *Guanabo* and Atlantic Ocean

External links

- Town info [1] (Spanish)

Geographical coordinates: 23°09′53″N 82°08′21″W

Things to See and Do

Havana Museum of Decorative Arts

The **Museum of Decorative Arts** (*Museo de Artes Decorativas*), in the Vedado district of Havana, Cuba it's a decorative arts museum in the former residence of the Maria Luisa Gomez Mena viuda de Cagiga, *Countess of Revilla de Camargo*, sister of Jose Gomez Mena, the owner of the Manzana de Gomez. It was it was designed in Paris by architects P. Virad and M. Destuque, inspired in French Renaissance and was built between 1924 and 1927 in a neo-classical style.

Address

Calle 17 #502, between E and D, Vedado, Havana, Cuba

References

- *Cuba - Eyewitness Travel Guides* (Dorling Kindersley Publishing, 2004) ISBN: 075660172X
- *Havana* (Lonely Planet Publications,2001) ISBN: 1864502290

Museo del Aire (Cuba)

Museo del Aire *(Aircraft: Antonov An-2)*	

Established	17 April 1986
Location	Ciudad de La Habana (Havana), Cuba
Type	Aviation museum

The **Museo del Aire** is a national aviation museum located in the south-western suburbs of Havana, Cuba. The Museum address is: Museo del Aire, Avenida 212, entre la avenida 29 y 31, La Coronela, La Lisa.

Aircraft on display

Source: Ogden

Designation	Identity	Notes
Aero L-39C Albatros	16	
Antonov An-2	I-40	
Antonov An-26	T-53	
CCF Harvard 4	116	
Cessna 310C	58	
Douglas A-26B Invader	937	
Ilyushin Il-14	CU-T825	Cubana de Aviación
Lockheed T-33A	703	
MiG-15UTI	02	
MiG-17F	237	

MiG-19P	88	
MiG-21F13	411	
MiG-21MF	111	
MiG-21PF	1006	
MiG-21UM	502	
MiG-23BN	711	
MiG-23MF	822	
MiG-23ML	223	
MiG-23UB	706	
Mil Mi-4P	H-100	
Mil Mi-8T	H-02	
Mil Mi-8TB	H-85	
Mil Mi-17	101	
Mil Mi-24D	12	
P-51D Mustang	401	
T-28A Trojan	121	
Yakovlev Yak-40	14-41	

See also

- Museo de la Revolución
- List of aerospace museums

References

- Ogden, Bob (2008). Aviation Museums and Collections of The Rest of the World. UK: Air-Britain. ISBN 9780851303949

External links

- MuseumAviation.eu: *Museo_del_Aire* [1]

Geographical coordinates: 23°4′5″N 82°27′30″W

Museo Nacional de Bellas Artes de La Habana

The **National Museum of Fine Arts of Havana (Museo Nacional de Bellas Artes de La Habana)** in Havana, Cuba is a museum of Fine Arts that exhibits Cuban art collections from the colonial times up to contemporary generations. It was founded on February 23, 1913 due to the efforts of its first director, Emilio Heredia, a well-known architect. After frequent moves it was finally placed on the block once occupied by the old Colon Market. In 1954, a new Palacio of Bellas Artes was opened, designed by the architect Rodriguez Pichardo. The original 1954 Palacio was recently reconstructed by the architect Jose Linares and a second building was taken over for the Museum.

There are now two impressive buildings belonging to the Museum, one dedicated to Cuban Arts in the *Palacio de Bellas Artes* (*Palace of Fine Arts*) and one dedicated to the Universal Arts, in the *Palacio del Centro Asturiano* (*Palace of the Asturian Center*).

The *Palacio de Bellas Artes* (*Palace of Fine Arts*) is dedicated exclusively to housing Cuba Art collections. Spanning the 17th and 19th centuries has rooms devoted to landscape, religious subjects and the Costumbrismo narrative scenes of Cuban life. Gallery devoted to the 1970s is marked by a preponderance of Hyperrealism and the latest generation of Cuban artists whose works all reflect the strong symbolic imagery that has been prevalent in recent decades. The most notable works are those of René Portocarrero and Wifredo Lam. A modernist sculpture by noted Cuban artist Rita Lonja stands outside the main entrance.

In the *Palacio del Centro Asturiano* (*Palace of the Asturian Center*) built in 1927 by the architect Manuel Bustos European paintings and sculptures, along with a collection of ancient art are on displayed there. Originally, it was a club for natives of the Spanish Province of Asturias and after the 1959 Revolution it housed the Supreme Court of Justice.

Asturian Center in 1927

Address

- Palace of Fine Arts - Trocadero Street e/Zulueta y Monserrate, Old Havana, Havana, Cuba 10200
- Palace of the Asturian Center - San Rafael, e/Zulueta y Monserrate, Old Havana, Havana, Cuba 10200

External links

- Museo Nacional de Bellas Artes de La Habana web page [1]

References

- *Cuba - Eyewitness Travel Guides* (Dorling Kindersley Publishing, 2004) ISBN 075660172X
- *Moon Handbooks: Cuba' (Avalon Travel Publishing, 2007) ISBN 1566918022*
- *The Odyssey Illustrated Guide To Cuba* (Guidebook Company Ltd. , 1995) ISBN 9622173705

Geographical coordinates: 23°8′24.8″N 82°21′25.9″W

Museum of the Revolution

The **Museum of the Revolution** (Spanish: *Museo de la Revolución*) is a museum located in the Old Havana section of Havana, Cuba. The museum is housed in what was the *Presidential Palace* of all Cuban presidents from Mario García Menocal to Fulgencio Batista. It became the Museum of the Revolution during the years following the Cuban revolution.

Building

The former *Presidential Palace* was designed by the Cuban architect Carlos Maruri and the Belgian architect Paul Belau and was inaugurated in 1920 by President Mario García Menocal. It remained the *Presidential Palace* until 1959. The building has Neo-Classical elements, and was decorated by Tiffany & Co. of New York.

Exhibits

The museum's Cuban history exhibits are largely devoted to the period of the revolutionary war of the 1950s and to the country's post-1959 history. Portions of the museum are also devoted to pre-revolutionary Cuba, including its War of Independence waged against Spain.

Behind the building lies the Granma Memorial, a large glass enclosure which houses the *Granma*, the yacht which took Fidel Castro and his revolutionaries from Mexico to Cuba for the revolution. Around the Granma an SA-2 Guideline surface-to-air missile of the type that shot down a U.S. Lockheed U-2 spyplane during the Cuban Missile Crisis, and the engine of the U-2 airplane is displayed. There are also various vehicles and tanks used in the revolution displayed. Near the museum is located an SU-100, a Soviet tank destroyer.

Gallery

Che Guevara and Camilo Cienfuegos guns and caps

Arnaldo Tamayo Méndez's space suit

Fulgencio Batista's gold-plated telephone

Hawker Sea Fury F50 at the museum

SU-100 at the museum

External links

- The Museo de la Revolución's home page (In Spanish) [1]
- English travel guide to the Museum of the Revolution [2]

Geographical coordinates: 23°08′30″N 82°21′24″W

Real Fabrica de Tabacos Partagás

The **Real Fabrica de Tabacos Partagás** is a cigar factory museum in Havana, Cuba. The world famous Habanos cigars are produced in this factory. Across the street from the massive Capitol building in Havana, is one of Cuba's oldest cigar factories. The Real Fabrica de Tabacos Partagas is housed in a well preserved industrial building dating from 1845. The building stands out amongst its peers because of the ornate colorful maroon and cream exterior. Real Fabrica de Tabacos Partagas was started by Jaime Partagas but foundered after his mysterious death. Ramon Cifuentes took over and the business grew under his stewardship.

The factory

Gallery

External links

- Partagas Factory & Cigar Sign Video [1]
- Partagas Celebrates 150 Years at the Same Address [2]

Cathedral of Havana

The **Catedral de San Cristóbal de La Havana** (Cathedral of Saint Christopher of Havana) is a Roman Catholic Cathedral and is the seat of Jaime Lucas Ortega y Alamino, the Cardinal Archbishop of Havana, Cuba. It was constructed by Jesuits (1748–77) on the site of an earlier church.

Set in the former Plaza de La Ciénaga or Swamp Plaza, the Cathedral is said to be the only example of a baroque facade that was designed with asymmetrical features - one of the towers is wider than the other. This particular feature was conceived in order to allow the water that tended to accumulate on the plaza to freely flow through the streets during the colonial period, when it was built.

Cuban writer Alejo Carpentier famously described the Cathedral as "music set in stone". It is the most prominent building on the Plaza de la Catedral, in Old Havana.

Photo gallery

External links

- Havana puts on New Face for Pope [1] by Phillip True, *Express News*, January 21 1998
- "San Cristóbal Cathedral" picture gallery [2] at Remains.se

Geographical coordinates: 23°08′28.97″N 82°21′06.90″W

Basilica Menor de San Francisco de Asis

The **basilica and the monastery of San Francisco de Asis** (Saint Francis of Assisi) were built in Havana, Cuba at the end of sixteenth century (1580-91) as the home of the Franciscan community, and were altered in the baroque style in 1730.

The church was used for their worship by the English during the year in which they ruled Havana. When it returned to Spanish rule, they chose not to use it as a church. It is now used for concerts. Attached to the Basilica is a bell tower (138-ft). Originally a statue of St. Francis of Assisi stood on the top of the bell tower but it was destroyed by a cyclone in 1846. Today a statue of St. Francis and a boy stand next to the basilica.

"El Caballero de Paris" statue by Jose Maria Lopez-Lledin. The metal statue's beard has been polished over the years by the hands of tourists and seekers of good luck.

The cloister of the adjacent monastery which dates back to 1739 now houses a museum of holy art. In front of the Basilica on the sidewalk stands a bronze life-size statue by Jose Villa Soberon of José María López Lledín known as *El Caballero de Paris* (1899-1985) who is buried inside the Basilica.

External links

- Iglesia San Francisco [1]
- Church Nave [2]
- Convent Gardens [3]

References

- *Cuba - Eyewitness Travel Guides* (Dorling Kindersley Publishing, 2004) ISBN: 075660172X
- *Havana* (Lonely Planet Publications,2001) ISBN: 1864502290
- *The Odyssey Illustrated Guide To Cuba* (Guidebook Company Ltd. , 1995) ISBN: 9622173705

Iglesia de Jesús de Miramar

Iglesia de Jesús de Miramar is the second largest church in Cuba. It is located in the Roman Catholic Archdiocese of San Cristobal de la Habana. It was begun in 1948 and inaugurated on May 28, 1953. It is done in Roman-Byzantine style. Its architect was Eugenio Cosculluela y Barreras.

The murals in the church were painted by the Spanish painter, Cesareo Marciano Hombrados y de Onativia (1909–1977) between the years 1952 and 1959. There are more than 266 figures represented in the 14 large murals. His model for the Virgin Mary was his wife, Sara Margarita Fernandez y Lopez (born August 5, 1927 in Havana, Cuba).

The largest pipe organ in Cuba (with 5000 tubes) was inaugurated on November 22, 1956. Parts of the organ was brought from Spain and the rest was constructed in the Church by the Spaniard, Guillermo de Aizpura.

In the gardens of the Church grounds is a copy of the Grotto of the Virgin of Our Lady of Lourdes, France designed by the architect Max Borges Jr. and inaugurated on May 13, 1958. The church is located at Quinta Ave esquina a 82, Miramar, La Habana, Cuba.

References

- *Cuba - Eyewitness Travel Guides* (Dorling Kindersley Publishing, 2004) ISBN 075660172X
- *Havana* (Lonely Planet Publications,2001) ISBN 1864502290
- *The Odyssey Illustrated Guide To Cuba* (Guidebook Company Ltd. , 1995) ISBN 9622173705

Geographical coordinates: 23°06′20.55″N 82°26′27.82″W

Beth Shalom Temple (Havana, Cuba)

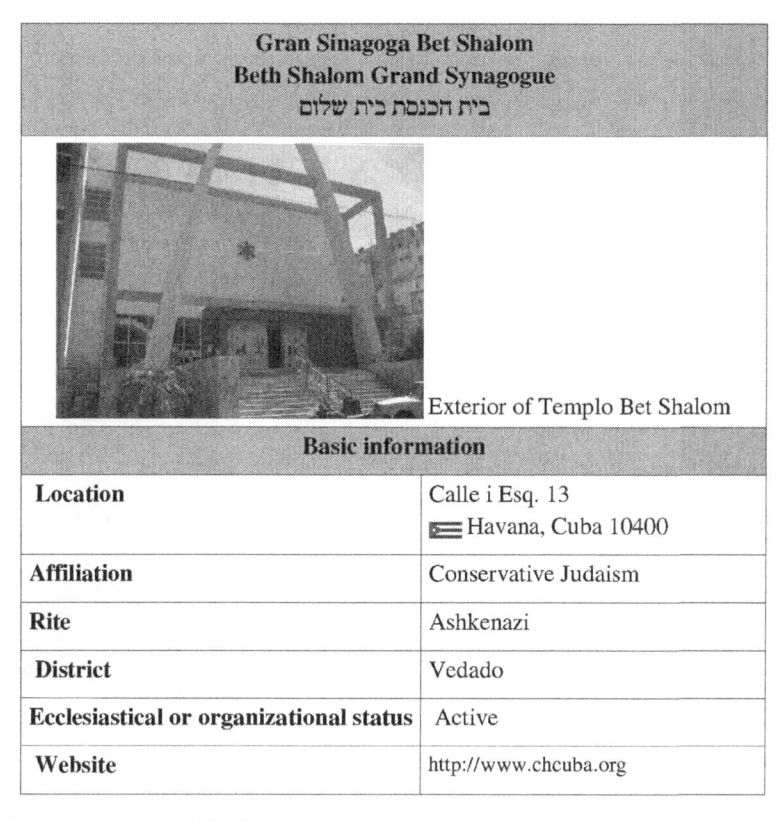

Gran Sinagoga Bet Shalom
Beth Shalom Grand Synagogue
בית הכנסת בית שלום

Exterior of Templo Bet Shalom

Basic information	
Location	Calle i Esq. 13 Havana, Cuba 10400
Affiliation	Conservative Judaism
Rite	Ashkenazi
District	Vedado
Ecclesiastical or organizational status	Active
Website	http://www.chcuba.org

Temple Beth Shalom, built in 1957, is a synagogue located near downtown Havana.

References

Geographical coordinates: 23°08′30″N 82°23′22″W

Plaza de la Catedral

Plaza de la Catedral (English: *Place of the Cathedral*) is a cathedral in Cuba built by Roman Catholic priests. The cathedral is an example for Spanish architecture in the Spanish colonies.

Palacio de los Capitanes Generales

The **Palacio de los Capitanes Generales** is the former official residence of the governors (Captains General) of Havana, Cuba. Located on the eastern side of the Plaza de Armas in Old Havana it is home to the Museum of the City of Havana (*Museo de la Ciudad*). It houses exhibitions of art and historical artefacts and many of the rooms are preserved with their original Colonial decoration.

The galleried upper storey of the Palacio de los Capitanes Generales looks down onto a central courtyard.

History

The plan for the building was put forward to the city council on 28 January 1773 by the governor Felipe de Fondesviela y Ondeano, marqués de la Torre. He proposed that the Parroquial Mayor church be demolished, the square be redesigned in keeping with the grandeur of the developing city and the Palacio de los Capitanes Generales constructed on the eastern side of the square in imitation of Royal Post Office (which would later become the Palacio del Segundo Cabo, the residence of the vice-governors) which had been constructed on the northern side of the square alongside the Castillo de la Real Fuerza. Construction from the designs of the Cuban engineer and architect, Antonio Fernández de Trebejos y Zaldívar, who had already been responsible for the much-admired post office, commenced in 1776. Much of the material used in the construction was imported to ensure it was of the finest quality: the bricks from Málaga, wrought-iron grilles from Bilbao and marble from Genoa, but the building work was carried out by slaves and progressed so slowly that the new governor (the sixth since de Fondesviela), Luís de las Casas y Arragorri, was not able to occupy the building until 1791, and work was not completed until 1792. The building originally housed the governor's residence and a prison, as well as being used as the meeting place for the city council, as the original council offices in Plaza San Francisco had been badly damaged by a hurricane in 1768. The prison, located in the west wing, was closed in 1834.

The last of the Colonial governors vacated the palace in 1898 when Cuba gained independence under the terms of the Treaty of Paris, and it was used by the US military governors from 1899 until 1902. It was used as the presidential palace of the Cuban Republic from 1902 until 1920, when the president relocated to the building which now houses the Museum of the Revolution and the Palacio de los Capitanes Generales became once again the offices of the city council. The municipal authorities moved elsewhere in 1967 and in 1968 the palace became the City Museum.

Building

The building is in the Cuban Baroque style. It is a thick-walled square building, little altered from the time of its original construction. The front of the building has an arcade with arches supported by columns and a pavement made from *china pelona*. Above the arcade the first storey has a limestone façade created from local limestone, notable for the numerous marine fossils embedded in the stone. Small balconies extend out from the full length stained-glass windows, level with the top of the columns below. In the centre of the building is an open leafy courtyard overlooked by a gallery on all four sides.

The ground floor and mezzanine contain artwork and artefacts from Havana's past. "La Giradilla", a statue that became symbol of the city, and was originally located on the tower of the nearby Castillo de la Real Fuerza, stands at the foot of the stairs leading to the mezzanine. The Cenotaph, the oldest colonial monument in Cuba, taken from the original Parroquial Mayor church, is on display in one of the rooms on the lower floor, and another room houses relics from the Espada Cemetery, including the tomb of the French artist Jean Baptiste Vermay. The Espada Cemetery was the first cemetery in the city, founded by Juan José Diaz de Espada in 1806. Also on display are some of the original stone baths in the shape of a nautilus shell and a 19th-century fire engine manufactured in London.

On the top floor the rooms of the governor's residence are preserved with much of the original furniture and decoration. The Hall of Heroic Cuba contains important objects from the wars of independence and many flags of national significance including the flag of Carlos Manuel de Céspedes, the "Father of the Homeland" (*Padre de la Patria*). The building also houses the Office of the City Historian, headed by Eusebio Leal, which is responsible for the renovation work in Old Havana.

References

- Barclay, Juliet (2003). *Havana: Portrait of a City*. Cassell Illustrated. pp. 224. ISBN 1844031276.
- "World Heritage List: Old Havana and its Fortifications" [1]. UNESCO. 1982. Retrieved 30 March 2007.
- Rachel Carley (2000). *Cuba: 400 Years of Architectural Heritage*. Watson-Guptill. p. 224. ISBN 0823011283.

El Capitolio

El_Capitolio.jpg Main steps leading up to the portico	
Architectural style	Neo-classical, art nouveau
Town	Havana
Country	Cuba
Started	April 1, 1926
Completed	May 20, 1929
Cost	17 million pesos (at the time)
Architect	Raúl Otero and Eugenio Raynieri

El Capitolio, or **National Capitol Building** in Havana, Cuba, was the seat of government in Cuba until after the Cuban Revolution in 1959, and is now home to the Cuban Academy of Sciences. Its design and name recall the United States Capitol in Washington, D.C., but it is only superficially similar. Completed in 1929, it was the tallest building in Havana until the 1950s and houses the world's third largest indoor statue.

History

The site occupied by El Capitolio was originally an area of swamp which was later used for slave dwellings and later still for the country's first botanical garden. In 1839, after the plants were relocated, the Villanueva Station (*Estación de Ferrocarriles de Villanueva*) was constructed on the site. The station was inaugurated in 1839 and was in use until the first decade of the 20th century when a modern station was constructed further to the east of the city. Before the existing building was erected there were other construction projects proposed for the site. The first, proposed in 1912, was to build a Presidential Palace, but the idea was later modified to construction of a building for the Cuban legislature. Financing was obtained and the work started in December 1917 but stopped during World War I and was never recommenced. The dome of the building, which had been completed before work was suspended, was destroyed in an explosion in 1918.

View from a nearby building

In 1925, the dictator Gerardo Machado took power and commissioned a new design from the architects Raúl Otero and Eugenio Raynieri. The previous, partially completed building was demolished and work began on the new building on 1 April 1926. Over seen by the U.S. firm of Purdy and Henderson, 8,000 labourers worked 8-hour shifts 24 hours a day, and as a result the building was completed in just 3 years and 50 days.

The building was named after a referendum on the choice of either the *El Palacio del Congreso* (*Palace of Congress*) or *El Capitolio*, and was inaugurated on 20 May 1929. The legislature did not move into the building until February 1931, as although the structure was complete by 1929 it took almost another two years before the interior decoration was finished. The building is finished with fine marble throughout and the total cost of construction and decoration is estimated to have been 17 million pesos. The building served as the seat of the legislature until the late 1950s; both the House of Representatives and Senate were based in the building. In the 1960s it became home to the Ministry of Science, Technology and the Environment. The main floor (which is on the first storey) is open to visitors and many of the rooms are used to host conferences and meetings.

Building

The neoclassical building is strongly reminiscent of the U.S. Capitol, but Raynieri claimed to take his inspiration for the cupola from the Panthéon in Paris.

The cupola, which is stone clad around a steel frame which was constructed in the United States and imported to Cuba, is set forward on the building to allow for some large rooms at the rear, including what is now the National Library of Science and Technology. In the original design the dome was to be decorated with stylised palm leaves but this addition was never executed. At almost 92 m (300 ft) high, the dome was the highest point in the city of Havana until the 1950s (this honour now belongs to the José Martí Memorial).

Around the building are gardens laid out by French landscape architect and designer Jean-Claude Nicolas Forestier at the time of the original construction. Based on the designs of some of the beautiful simple European gardens they consist of areas of lawn bordered by paths and highlighted by palms. Four groups of Royal Palms accent the design.

La Estatua de la República, the world's third largest statue under cover

The 55 steps leading to the main entrance, known as *La Escalinata* are flanked on either side by 6.5 m (21 ft) statues by the Italian artist Angelo Zanelli. To the left is *Work* (*El Trabajo*) and to the right *The Tutelary Virtue* (*La Virtud Tutelar*). The steps lead up to the central portico, which is 36 m (118 ft) wide and more than 16 m (52½ ft) tall. There are 12 granite Roman style columns arranged in two rows and each over 14 m (46 ft) tall. Beyond the portico, three large bronze doors with bas-reliefs by Zanelli allow access to the main hall.

The inside of the main hall under the cupola is dominated by the huge *Statue of the Republic* (*La Estatua de la República*). The statue, also by Zanelli, was cast in bronze in Rome in three pieces and assembled inside the building after its arrival in Cuba. It is covered with 22 carat (92 %) gold leaf and weighs 49 tons. At 15 m (49¼ ft) tall, it was the second highest statue under cover in the world at the time, with only the Great Buddha of Nara being taller. It was later relegated to third place after the construction of the statue of Abraham Lincoln in the Lincoln Memorial. The statue stands on a plinth 2.5 m (8¼ ft) high bringing the total height to 17.54 m (55¼ ft). A Creole Cuban, Lily Valty served as the model for the body for Zanelli, and the inspiration for the statue came from Athena, the Greek goddess of wisdom.

Embedded in the floor in the centre of the main hall is a replica 25 carat (5 g) diamond, which marks Kilometre Zero for Cuba. The original diamond, said to have belonged to Tsar Nicholas II of Russia and have been sold to the Cuban state by a Turkish merchant, was stolen on 25 March 1946 and mysteriously returned to the President, Ramón Grau San Martín, on 2 June 1946. It was replaced in El Capitolio by a replica in 1973.

To either side of the main hall is the *Salón de Pasos Perdidos* (*Hall of Lost Steps*), named for its acoustic properties. These halls, with inlaid marble floors and gilded lamps, lead to the two semicircular chambers that formerly housed the Parliament and Chamber of Deputies. The Parliament chamber to the right of building is backed on to by the President's office which has a door opening directly onto the dias.

A range of different lamps are seen throughout the building. These were all designed specifically for the building by Cuban designers and the majority of them manufactured in France.

In the centre of the building are two patios which provide light and ventilation for the offices of first (ground), third and fourth floors. The north patio features another statue *The Rebellious Angel* (*El Ángel Rebelde*) which was donated to the building after the inauguration. There is a small fifth floor, and a sixth floor which gives access only to part of the cupola.

Images

Work, one of two statues by Angelo Zanelli which flank the central steps

The Tutelary Virtue, the companion to *Work*

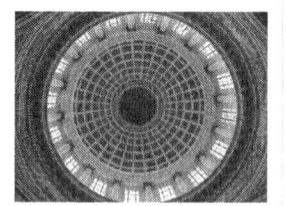

The interior of the cupola

The replica diamond at Kilometre Zero inside El Capitolio

Salón de los Pasos Perdidos

El Capitolio

Inside view of El Capitolio
La Habana

Geographical coordinates: 23°08′07″N 82°21′34″W

References

- "El Capitolio de la Habana" [1] (in Spanish). Convenciones Capitolio de La Habana. 2007. Retrieved 3 May 2007.
- Rachel Carley (2000). *Cuba: 400 Years of Architectural Heritage*. Watson-Guptill. p. 224. ISBN 0823011283.
- "Capitolio de La Habana" [2] (in Spanish). Retrieved 3 May 2007.
- Pedro Quiroga (1998). "El Capitolio: Un emporio en La Habana" [3] (in Spanish). Radio Reloj, La Habana. Retrieved 3 May 2007.

La Mansion

La Mansión de Mark Pollack, is a neo-classical Florentine mansion in the Cubanacan Section (fka Country Club section) of Havana, Cuba built in 1930 by the Cuban architect, Leonardo Morales y Pedroso (1887–1965). It is located at 21st street #15001, Cubanacan, Havana, Cuba.

La Mansión de Mark Pollack in 1931.

It was built for Mark Alexander Pollack (1874–1946),the son of Alexander Pollack and Isabella A. Rothschild (1848-1936), the American born patriarch of a wealthy Cuban tobacco exporters and covers an area of 13,000 square meters.

It is one of the crown jewels of Cuban architecture and one of the most significant work of Cuban Eclecticism due to its temperate lines, and ornaments with no parallel in the modern and contemporary architecture. It has large rooms and is surrounded by extensive gardens, which in the past were arranged in a formal manner. Mr. Pollack, painted a series of panels referring to the discovery of America which were placed around the main hall, but due to the deteriorated state of them when the Cuban government decided to restore the home, they were lost forever.

This hall is extraordinary due to its size (approximately 48 feet (15 m) long and 24 feet (7.3 m) wide and high), the organ which took up one of its ends, the wooden balcony placed at half the height of the other end, and the iron grilles which lead to the portico, which is the main element of the facade facing the garden. This portico has three arcades supported by double columns and a richly decorated arched ceiling. The central courtyard is exceptional for Cuban house architecture in the 20th century, due to its size and the fact that it is completely surrounded by a porticoed gallery, the columns of which are all different kind of marble on both floors.

The mansion has been featured in Architectural Digest, *Six Days in Havana* by James A. Michener, was also featured in Maria Luisa Lobo Montalvo's "Havana", was the cover picture for Michael Connors' book "Cuban Elegance", was also the cover for "I Was Cuba: Treasures from the Ramiro Fernandez Collection" by Kevin Kwan, and is featured in dozens of other books celebrating Cuban architecture.

The property was leased to the Brazilian Embassy until Brazil broke relations with the Castro government, after which it was abandoned and allowed to deteriorate. In the 1990s, it was restored to its original splendor at a cost of over $2,000,000 and is now rented by the Cuban government for its important guests.

References

- *Inside Cuba* (Taschen, Spain 2006 ISBN 3-8228-4597-3)
- *Havana, Cuba: An Architectural Guide* (A.G. Novograf, S.A., 1998, ISBN 84-8095-143-5)
- *Cuban Elegance* (Harry N. Abrams, 2004, ISBN 0810943379)
- *Havana: History and Architecture of a Romantic City* (Monacelli Press, 2000, ISBN 1580930522)
- *La Habana Arquitectura del Siglo XX*, Eduardo Luis Rodriguez (Blume, 2001) ISBN 978-8489396173 (Spanish)

External links

- Photographs of "La Mansion" [1]
- Cuban government advertisement for rental of "La Mansion" [2]

José Martí Memorial

José Martí Memorial	
General information	
Location	Havana, Cuba
Coordinates	23°07′22″N 82°23′12″W
Status	Complete
Constructed	1953 - 1958
Height	
Top floor	109 m (358 ft)
Companies involved	
Architect(s)	Enrique Luis Varela

The **José Martí Memorial** (Spanish: *Monumento a José Martí*) is a memorial to José Martí, the national hero of Cuba, located on the northern side of the Plaza de la Revolución in the Vedado area of Havana. It consists of a star-shaped tower, a statue of Martí surrounded by six columns, and gardens.

The 109 m (358 ft) tower, designed by a team of architects led by Enrique Luis Varela, is in the form of a five-pointed star, encased in grey Cuban marble from the Isla de la Juventud. The design was eventually selected from various entries put forward from a series of competitions beginning in 1939. Entries included a version of the tower topped with a statue of Martí, and a monument similar to the Lincoln Memorial in Washington, D.C. with a statue of Martí seated within. The fourth competition held in 1943 resulted in the selection of a design by the architect Aquiles Maza and the sculptor Juan José Sicre. In order to proceed with construction of the monument, the Monserrat Hermitage, which occupied the proposed site, had to be demolished. Various impediments to the acquisition of the Hermitage by the state led to delays in the demolition and the start of building work, so by 1952 – when Fulgencio Batista seized power in a coup – work on the construction had still not begun.

Eager to garner popular support after seizing power, Batista committed to pushing ahead with the construction of a monument to Martí; but rather than proceeding with the competition winner, he selected the design that had come third in the competition, created by a group of architects headed by Enrique Luis Varela, Batista's Minister of Works and his personal friend. The selection of this design caused something of a public outcry, and as a result the design was modified to remove the statue from the top of the tower, and to instead feature Juan José Sicre's statue of Marti at the foot of the tower. Construction of the tower began in 1953 on the 100th anniversary of José Martí's birth. The right to compensation for local inhabitants forced to move to make way for construction caused further problems; their case was taken up by a young Fidel Castro. The monument was finally completed in 1958 during the final days of the Batista dictatorship.

The selected design includes an enclosed observation deck on the top floor, the highest point in Havana, accessible by elevator which gives commanding views over the city in all directions. Housed on the ground floor of the tower which overlooks the city, the memorial features two rooms of correspondence, writings and items from the life of José Martí and displays relating his life story. A third room illustrates the history of the Plaza de la Revolucion, and a fourth room is used for displays of contemporary art. The centre of the tower houses the elevator and features walls decorated with quotes from Martí. Among other items on display is a replica of the sword of Simón Bolívar presented to Fidel Castro by Hugo Chávez during his visit to Cuba in 2002.

Outside, facing over the plaza and towards the mural of Che Guevara on the Ministry of the Interior on the opposite side of the square, is an 18 m (59 ft) white marble statue of Martí carved *in situ* by Sicre and surrounded by six half-height marble columns. The platform where the statue is located is used as a podium when rallies take place in the Plaza de la Revolución.

Gallery

Sicre's Statue of Martí.

As of January 16, 2005.

References

- "Historia del memorial" [1] (in Spanish). Memorial José Martí. Archived from the original [2] on 3 February 2007. Retrieved 26 March 2007.
- Information from Memorial José Martí. Retrieved 26 March 2007

External links

- JoséMartí.cu Portal José Martí [1] (Spanish)

La Cabaña

The **Fortaleza de San Carlos de la Cabaña**, commonly known simply as **La Cabaña**, is an 18th century fortress complex, the biggest in the Americas, located on the elevated eastern side of the harbor entrance in Havana, Cuba.

Construction of La Cabaña was begun in 1763 by King Carlos III of Spain, the controlling colonial power of Cuba, following the recent capture of Havana by British forces (an exchange was soon made to give Cuba back to the Spanish in exchange for Florida). Realising that the city was not well enough defended and fearing further attacks following British colonial conquests in the Seven Years War they now moved to build a new fortress to boost the defence of Havana. Replacing earlier fortifications next to the 16th century El Morro fortress, La Cabaña was the largest colonial military installation in the New World by the time it was completed in 1774, at great expenses to Spain; so much the King proclaimed it should be visible from Spain having cost so much and take so long to be finished.

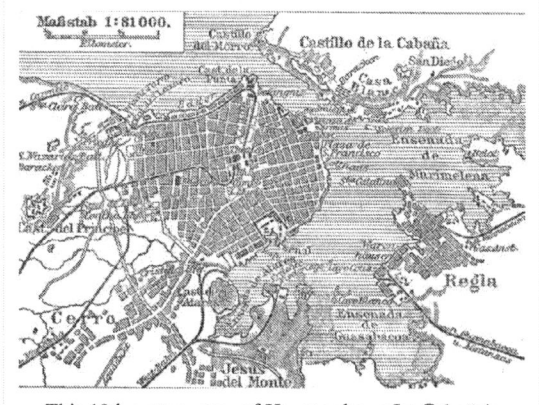

This 19th century map of Havana shows La Cabaña's strategic location along the east side of the entrance to the city's harbor.

The fortress served as both a military base and prison over the next two hundred years for both Spain and an independent Cuba. La Cabaña was used as a military prison during the Batista regime. In January 1959, rebels led by Che Guevara captured La Cabaña and used it as a headquarters and as a military prison for several months while leading the Cuban revolution. During his five-month tenure in that post (January 2 through June 12, 1959), Guevara oversaw the revolutionary tribunals and executions of suspected war criminals, traitors, *chivatos* (informants), and former members of Batista's secret police. The complex is now part of a historical park, along with El Morro, and houses several museums open to the public. From there, every night a cannon shot rumbles at 9pm so called "El Cañonazo de las 9", a custom, kept from colonial times, signaling the closure of the city wall doors.

Gallery

The fortress walls.

An administrative office. Supposedly, Che Guevara commanded the fortress from here during the Cuban Missile Crisis.

An avenue between buildings of the fortress.

External links

- "History of Havana's Fortress Cabana" [1].

Geographical coordinates: 23°08′50″N 82°21′00″W

Castillo de la Real Fuerza

The **Castillo de la Real Fuerza** (Castle of the Royal Force) is a fortress on the western side of the harbour in Havana, Cuba, set back from the entrance, and bordering the Plaza de Armas. Originally built to defend against attack by pirates, it suffered from a poor strategic position too far inside the bay. The fortress is considered to be the oldest stone fortress in the Americas, and was listed in 1982 as part of the UNESCO World Heritage site of "Old Havana and its Fortifications".

Castillo de la Real Fuerza.

History

A previous fortress, the Fuerza Vieja (Old Force), was badly damaged in 1555 during an attack on Havana by the French privateer Jacques de Sores and eventually was demolished in 1582. In 1558 Bartolomé Sánchez, an engineer appointed by King Philip II of Spain, began work on the new fortress, initially known as the *Fuerza Nueva* (New Force). The Fuerza Vieja was set back from the harbour, but the new fortress was planned to be closer to the harbour to give it a better strategic position. The ironworks were established in 1558, but the first stones were not laid until 1562. Construction was delayed due to complaints from local residents forced to relocate to make way for the building and from disagreements between Sánchez and the Governor of Havana. The fortress was not completed until 1577, with slaves and French prisoners providing most of the labour. Built of limestone quarried from the Havana shoreline, the fortification incorporated thick sloping walls, a moat and drawbridge. The governor, Francisco Carreño, ordered the addition an upper storey as barracks and a munitions store, but on completion, the fortress proved to be too small for practical use.

Despite being positioned closer to the harbour than the Fuerza Vieja, it quickly became apparent that the new fortress was still too distant from the mouth of the harbour to serve effectively as a defensive bulwark, so was instead adopted by Juan de Tejeda as the residence of the Governor of Havana. Subsequent governors made changes to the building, and in 1634, Juan Vitrián de Viamonte added a watchtower with a weathervane sculpted in the form of a woman, by Gerónimo Martín Pinzón, an artist from Havana, and based on the figure crowning La Giralda in Seville. Although the reason for the

A view of the watchtower from the outside

choice of this figure, called La Giraldilla, is not known, a common suggestion is to honour Inés de Bobadilla, Havana's only female governor, who assumed control from her husband Hernando de Soto when he undertook an expedition to Florida. She spent many years scanning the horizon for signs of his returning ship (unbeknown to her, he had died). The figure became the symbol of the city of Havana (it features on the Havana Club rum label), and is now held at the City Museum housed in the Palacio de los Capitanes Generales in the Plaza de Armas, while a copy is in place on the watchtower. The façade of the fortress was demolished in 1851 to allow O'Reilly Street to go all the way to the docks, and prevent El Templete, completed in 1828, from being overshadowed by the fortress.

Use

The fortress was home to the National Archive from 1899 and the National Library from 1938 up until 1957, when both were relocated to a purpose-built library in Plaza de la Revolución. After the Cuban Revolution in 1959, it housed the offices the National Commission of Monuments and the Centre of Preservation, Restoration and Museology. Used briefly as the Museum of Arms, the conditions within the fortress were not conducive to the preservation of the displays. In 1977, on the 400th anniversary of completion, the building was inaugurated as a museum and used to display exhibitions of Cuban contemporary and international art. In 1990, it became the National Museum of Cuban Ceramics, but as of 2007, no displays are housed in the fortress. Some restoration work was carried out on the fortress prior to the inclusion of the fortification in the UNESCO World Heritage citation for Old Havana.

External links

- Independent visitors guide to the Castillo [1]

References

- "Castillo de la Real Fuerza (Castle of the Royal Force)" [2]. Old Havana Web. 2006. Retrieved 30 March 2007.
- "World Heritage List: Old Havana and its Fortifications" [1]. UNESCO. 1982. Retrieved 30 March 2007.
- Rachel Carley (2000). *Cuba: 400 Years of Architectural Heritage*. Watson-Guptill. p. 224. ISBN 0823011283.
- "Monumentos Nacionales: Habana Vieja" [3] (in Spanish). Consejo Nacional de Patrimonio Cultural. Retrieved 1 March 2007.

Geographical coordinates: 23°08′27.62″N 82°20′58.90″W

Castillo de San Pedro de la Roca

San Pedro de la Roca Castle, Santiago de Cuba*	
UNESCO World Heritage Site	
State Party	Cuba
Type	Cultural
Criteria	iv, v
Reference	841 [1]
Region**	Latin America and the Caribbean
Inscription history	
Inscription	1997 (21st Session)
* Name as inscribed on World Heritage List. [2] ** Region as classified by UNESCO. [3]	

The **Castillo de San Pedro de la Roca** (also known by the less formal title of **Castillo del Morro** or as **San Pedro de la Roca Castle**) is a fortress on the coast of the Cuban city of Santiago de Cuba. About 6 miles (10 km) southwest of the city centre, it overlooks the bay.Geographical coordinates: 19°58′7.34″N 75°52′13.08″W

History

Initial design

It was designed in 1637 by Giovan Battista Antonelli (also known as Juan Battista Antonelli), a member of a Milanese family of military engineers, on behalf of the governor of the city, Pedro de la Roca y Borja, as a defense against raiding pirates, although an earlier, smaller, fortification had been built between 1590 and 1610. Antonelli design was adapted to the situation of the fortress on the steep sides of the promontory (the *morro* from which the fortress gets its name) reaching into the bay. It was constructed on a series of terraces; there were four main levels and three large bulwarks to house the artillery. Supplies would be delivered by sea and then stored in the large warehouse, which was cut directly into the rock, or transported up to the top level which housed the citadel. Construction of the citadel took 42 years, starting in 1638 and finally being completed in 1700, though work on the fortification was spasmodic. Antonelli was recalled to Cuba in 1645, shortly after the massive project was started, and other examples of his work can be seen there in the twin forts of Fuerte del Cojimar and Fuerte de Santa Doratea de Luna de Chorrera. Some of the structures from the earlier fortification were later incorporated into the main structure.

Further construction

View over the bay from the fortress

The fear of pirate attacks was well-founded. While the fortress was still being constructed in 1662, English freebooters under the guidance of Christopher Myngs took control of Santiago for two weeks and during their stay destroyed part of the fortification and captured the artillery. After they departed, the Spanish government ordered the reconstruction of the damaged part of the fortress and raised the garrison to 300 men. Between 1663 and 1669 the engineers Juan Císcara Ibáñez, Juan Císcara Ramirez and Francisco Perez worked on repairing the damage and improving the fortifications, strengthening the flanks and constructing a new artillery platform. In 1678 it frustrated the attack of a French squadron and in 1680 fought off another attack by 800 men led by Franquesma, the second-in-command of the Antilles filibusters.

Between 1675 and 1692 the fortress was damaged by a series of earthquakes and reconstruction had to be carried out under the direction of Francisco Pérez between 1693 and 1695. From 1738-1740 further work was undertaken by the engineer Antonio de Arredondo, who enlarged the citadel and completed some of the unfinished platforms, with Juan Martín Cermeño and Francisco Calderín making the final changes to the structure after it was again damaged by earthquakes between 1757 and 1766.

By 1775, the fear of attack had diminished, and the parts of fortress known as the Rock (*la Roca*) and the Star (*la Estrella*) were converted into a prison for political prisoners, although the rest of the fortress continued to serve as a military base. It was again used as a fortress in 1898 when the United States' fleet attacked Santiago de Cuba during the Spanish-American War.

World Heritage Site

During the 20th century the Rock fell into decay, but it was restored during the 1960s by Francisco Prat Puig. The fortress was declared a World Heritage Site by UNESCO in 1997, cited as the best preserved and most complete example of Spanish-American military architecture.

References

- "World Heritage List: San Pedro de la Roca Castle, Santiago de Cuba" [1]. UNESCO. 1997. Retrieved 1 March 2007.
- Rachel Carley (2000). *Cuba: 400 Years of Architectural Heritage*. Watson-Guptill. p. 224. ISBN 0823011283.
- René Chartrand (2006). *The Spanish Main 1493-1800*. Osprey. pp. 64. ISBN 1846030056.
- "Monumentos Nacionales: Castillo de San Pedro de la Roca del Morro" [2] (in Spanish). Consejo Nacional de Patrimonio Cultural. Retrieved 1 March 2007.

Morro Castle (fortress)

Morro Castle Spanish: *Castillo de los Tres Reyes Magos del Morro*) is a picturesque fortress guarding the entrance to Havana bay in Havana, Cuba. Juan Bautista Antonelli, an Italian engineer, was commissioned to design the structure. When it was built in 1589, Cuba was under the control of Spain. The castle, named after the biblical Magi, was later captured by the British in 1762.

View of Havana from El Morro Castle

Morro Castle in Havana shares the name with other structures in Santiago de Cuba and the Castillo de San Felipe del Morro in San Juan, Puerto Rico.

Perched on the promontory on the opposite side of the harbor from Old Havana it can be viewed from miles around as it dominates the port entrance.

Built initially in 1589 in response to raids on Havana harbor, el Morro protected the mouth of the harbor with a chain being strung out across the water to the fort at La Punta.

Seven Years War

Main articles: Battle of Havana (1762) and Great Britain in the Seven Years War

It first saw action in the 1762 British expedition against Cuba when Lord Albemarle landed in Cojimar to the east of Havana, and attacked the fortress defended by Luis Vicente de Velasco e Isla from its landward side. It fell because the British successfully mined one of its bastions, so when they handed the island back in 1763 to Spain, the fortress at La Cabaña was built to prevent this from happening again.

Exhibition

Inside the gates is an exhibition on the lighthouses of Cuba – El Morro once housed a school for lighthouse keepers. There was actually a watchtower here until the British blew it up in their successful siege in 1762. The Faro Castillo del Morro lighthouse was added in 1846.

Havana Bay, c. 1639.

The cannons around the fort are now badly rusted but the walls are in great shape. The fort has central barracks up to four stories high. A small underwater archeology exhibition is also located here. Noteworthy are the old latrines and their chute into the sea as are the two sets of doors and the drawbridge mechanism. The current harbor master's office is still housed in the fortress. A plaque dedicated by the ambassador of the United Kingdom commemorates the 1762 siege and a small memorial is located between two strong powder rooms in the North East Bastion.

A small turret at the end of the wall offers views of the sea crashing onto the rocks 20 meters below and take in the dimensions of the huge dry moat. The opposite side of the moat holds more modern guns and cannons, La Bateria de Velasco, and offers a sweeping view down to Cojimar.

Gallery

El Morro

El Morro Castle seen from Havana.

Appearances

Seen on the McDougal Littell textbook *¡En español!* Level 2.

Morro Castle appears in the movie *The Ghost Breakers* (1940), in the background as Bob Hope and Paulette Goddard enter the harbor by ship.

During his life, the Cuban poet and novelist Reinaldo Arenas (1943-1990) was imprisoned at El Morro Castle by the Castro regime for his homosexuality. The film version of Arenas's autobiography, *Before Night Falls*, starring Javier Bardem, features scenes set in El Morro Castle prison. (A fortress in Mexico City doubled for the prison, since the filmmakers were not allowed to film in Cuba.)

References

There is a Cuban restaurant in Hialeah, FL named after the fortress

External links

Geographical coordinates: 23°09′01.67″N 82°21′23.99″W

San Salvador de la Punta Fortress

San Salvador de la Punta Fortress is a fortress in the bay of Havana, Cuba.

La Punta, just like El Morro was designed to protect the entrance to the Havana Bay that became an important and strategic entranceway to the harbor since the settlement of the town. The nonstop landings of corsairs in the area endangered the harbor and the town. That was why in 1559 it was resolved to post lookouts at La Punta.

In 1582 the king Felipe II, convinced that it was necessary to reinforce

fortresses and fleets, ordered the creation of a fortress system in several places of America having its center in Havana.

To fulfill the task Juan de Tejeda was appointed governor of the island, because of his expertise in the matter of fortifications. He brought along the Italian engineer Juan Bautista Antonelli, who has been considered the most renowned professional to practice in 16th century Cuba. The works began by 1590 and went on slowly. In 1595 a hurricane severely damaged the fortress, among other reasons, due to the thinness of its walls that were then more solidly rebuilt. By 1602 there was such a delay in the construction work that the engineer decided to make the fortress into a keep holding some 10 to 12 artillery pieces. Finally, as the years went by it was taken apart, leaving just 3 bastions.

In 1630, due to the short distance between La Punta and El Morro and to increase the protection of the bay, a heavy copper chain was laid between them. This chain can be appreciated in some of the engravings of that time.

In 1762 as a consequence of the fighting during the British expedition against Cuba, the English superiority took its toll on all the fortresses. The safety curtains and bastions of La Punta castle were destroyed during the invasion. At this time a chain branching out in several directions and held by heavy wood beams was laid. Its ends were tied to guns set-in at La Punta and El Morro. Some fragments of this piece still remain.

Later on, with the Spanish were back in power, a new governor arrived, fixing and enlarging the fortification system. In the 19th century some changes, such as the 4 esplanades built to accommodate a corresponding number of artillery pieces, were added at La Punta.

The castle, in 1997, was under an intense work of restoration, (by the City's Historian Office), that gave it its original position on the rocks. Thanks to this work canons that were engraved in the rocks. The park that surrounds it, paved with striking red ceramic tiles, is a memento of the San Antonio, a Spanish ship foundered in front of the castle with a heavy load. Some of the cargo was recovered from the flotsam and now gives the area just outside the building a special and highly distinctive character.

External links

- [1] Forts and Castles of the Caribbean Islands

Geographical coordinates: 23°08′46.51″N 82°21′27.79″W

Colon Cemetery, Havana

The **Colon Cemetery** or more fully in the Spanish language *Cementerio de Cristóbal Colón* was founded in 1876 in the Vedado neighbourhood of Havana, Cuba on top of Espada Cemetery. Named for Christopher Columbus, the 140 acre (57 ha) cemetery is noted for its many elaborately sculpted memorials. It is estimated that today the cemetery has more than 500 major mausoleums, chapels, and family vaults.

Colon Cemetery has a 75-foot (23 m)-high monument to the firefighters who lost their lives in the great fire of May 17, 1890. As baseball is

One of the many elaborate mausoleums inside the Colon Cemetery, Havana, Cuba

a leading sport in Cuba, the cemetery has two monuments to baseball players from the Cuban League. The first was erected in 1942 and the second in 1951 for members of the Cuban Baseball Hall of Fame.

In February 1898, the recovered bodies of sailors who died on the United States Navy battleship *Maine* were interred in the Colon

Cemetery. In December 1899 the bodies were disinterred and brought back to the United States for burial at Arlington National Cemetery. [1]

With more than 800,000 graves, space in the Colon Cemetery is currently at a premium and as such after three years remains are removed from their tombs, boxed and placed in a storage building. A few of the personalities interred here include:

- Santiago Álvarez (1919–1998), filmmaker
- Manuel Arteaga y Betancourt, Roman Catholic Cardinal
- Beatriz Azurduy Palacios (1952–2003), filmmaker
- Hubert de Blanck (1856–1932), composer
- José Raúl Capablanca (1888–1942), world chess champion
- Alejo Carpentier (1904–1980), novelist
- Eduardo Chibás (1907–1951), politician
- Juan Chabás (1910–1954), author
- Ibrahim Ferrer (1927–2005), musician
- Candelaria Figueredo (1852–1914), patriot in the Cuban struggle for independence from Spain

Main cemetery chapel located in the center of the cemetery

The northern main gate of the Colon Cemetery (Cementerio Cristóbal Colón) without the statues which were placed on the top in 1901

- José Miguel Gómez (1858–1921), president of Cuba
- Máximo Gómez (1836–1905), Dominican military hero
- Ruben Gonzalez (1919–2003), Cuban Pianist from Buena Vista Social Club
- Nicolás Guillén (1902–1989), poet
- Nicolás Guillén Landrián (1938–2003), Filmmaker and painter
- Tomás Gutiérrez Alea (1928–1996), filmmaker
- Harrison E. Havens (1837–1916), United States Congressman
- Alberto Korda (1928–2001), photographer
- José Lezama Lima (1910–1976), writer, poet
- Dulce María Loynaz (1902–1997), poet, novelist

- Dolf Luque (1890–1957), Major League Baseball starting pitcher
- Mary McCarthy Gomez Cueto (1900–2009), Havana socialite and musician
- Armando Marsans (1887–1960) Major League Baseball outfielder
- William Alexander Morgan (1928–1961), American adventurer
- Fernando Ortiz (1881–1969), ethnomusicologist
- German Pinelli (1907–1996), journalist, actor
- Chano Pozo (1915–1948), musician, pioneer of Afrocuban jazz
- Juan Ríus Rivera (1848–1924), Puerto Rican military hero
- Lola Rodríguez de Tió (1848–1924), Puerto Rican poetess.Car

External links

- Panoramic photo of Colon Cemetery [2]

Geographical coordinates: 23°07'23"N 82°23'55"W

El Templete

El Templete is a monument in Havana, Cuba, that pays homage to the place where the foundation of the town of San Cristóbal de la Habana was celebrated in 1519. The monument consists of bust of Christopher Columbus and three canvases painted by Jean Baptiste Vermay. It is Neoclassic building, typical example of colonial architecture.

Close to the Templete, there is a column which replaces a silk-cotton tree, under which the first mass and the first Council of Havana were celebrated.

Geographical coordinates: 23°08'25.78"N 82°20'56.52"W

Christ of Havana

The **Christ of Havana** is a large sculpture representing Jesus of Nazareth in Havana, Cuba. It is the work of the Cuban sculptor Jilma Madera.

The statue was carved out of Carrara marble, the same material used for many of the monuments of the Colon Cemetery. The statue is about 20 meters (66 ft) high and sits on a 3 meter base. It weighs approximately 320 tons. The statue was built from 67 blocks of marble that had been brought from Italy after being personally blessed by Pope Pius XII. The figure of Christ is standing with one hand held high and the other hand on his chest. Facing the city, the statue was left with empty eyes to give the impression of looking at all from anywhere to be seen.

The sculpture, located in the Havana suburb of Casablanca, in the municipality of Regla, was inaugurated on La Cabaña hill on December 24, 1958. Just fifteen days after its inauguration, on January 8, 1959, Fidel Castro entered Havana during the Cuban revolution. That same day, the image was hit by lightning and the head was destroyed. It was subsequently repaired.

The sculpture is located 51 meters (167 ft) above sea level[citation needed], allowing the locals to see it from many points of the city. There is a panoramic view point at the site of the sculpture.

José Martí Anti-Imperialist Plaza

The **José Martí Anti-Imperialist Plaza** opened across the street from the United States Interests Section in Havana in April 2000. It lies between the waterfront Malecón, Calzada Avenue and N and M streets on the coast of Havana. The first demonstration there was an anti-American protest over the custody of Elián González, a six year old Cuban boy at the time. This event was part of the Cuban efforts to have Elián returned to Cuba and his father, a movement that was ultimately successful in June that year. The site of the protest was just getting broken in, however, as it would be the grounds for dozens of government-led rallies in years to come. Information about the previous use of the land or the different construction projects on the land is scarce, however some important details can be seen in an aerial shot. For example, the design shown in the undated picture shows a giant star made into the ground, with the plaza's stage at the center. The red point of the star that points straight to the U.S. Interests Section building a few hundred feet away is most clear.Wikipedia:No original research

As of May 2006, the plaza includes a stage, metal arches over the crowd area, and a monument of 138 flags. The stage and arches have been up since before a May 2005 concert by the American rock band Audioslave, which the band claims was the first outdoor rock and roll concert on Cuban soil by an American band. The capacity of the plaza was an impressive 60,000 for that free concert, but the specifics as to the setup for each event are unknown.

The "Wall of Flags"

The flag monument by the plaza first appeared on February 6, 2006 as a response to and an obstruction of the American electronic message ticker on the fifth floor of the U.S. Interests building. The relationship between the monument and the ticker board is not coincidental, as evidenced by the flags' appearance less than a month after the billboard's first use on January 16 for the Martin Luther King, Jr. holiday. These 138 flags, each black with a white star in the center, were raised on 20 meter flagpoles, supposedly to put them high enough to block the ticker's visibility. Most likely, the flags will effectively block the audience in the José Martí Plaza from seeing the American ticker board, as they could during a speech by Fidel Castro in the plaza on January 24, 2006.

The number and design of the flags were to memorialize Cuban victims of terrorism, especially the 73 people who died in the 1976 bombing of a Cuban passenger airliner. When the flags were first hoisted in early February 2006, the alleged mastermind of this attack, Luis Posada Carriles, was under U.S. custody for illegal immigration to the U.S.

References

- http://www.radiohc.org/Distributions/Radio_Havana_English/.2000/2000_apr/ Radio_Havana_Cuba_News_-_4_April_2000
- http://havana.usinterestsection.gov/
- http://www.caribbeannetnews.com/cgi-script/csArticles/articles/000006/000652-p.htm
- http://www.walterlippmann.com/docs144.html
- Audioslave official website [1]

Related Pages

- José Martí
- United States Interests Section in Havana
- Audioslave
- Havana

Villa Marista

Villa Marista is a prison in Havana, Cuba, notorious for its detention of political prisoners by the Cuban national security agency.

Its prisoners have included poet Nicolas Guillén, dissident Vladimiro Roca, and politician Jesús Escandell.

Villa Marista school

Villa Marista originally prior to the Castro revolution a Catholic school for boys. The school was run by the Marist Brothers, and the name Marist was created by Marcellinus Champagnat the founder of the Marist Brothers; due to his faith and devotion to the Virgin Mary. Once the Castro Revolution expropriated the school and grounds from the Marist Brothers, the brothers were spread to other Marist schools around the world, including but not limited to Miami, Florida USA, Dominican Republic, Puerto Rico. In addition to the school in Havana the Marist Brothers also had another school in the city of Cienfuegos.

National Symphony Orchestra of Cuba

National Symphony Orchestra of Cuba (Spanish: *Orquesta Sinfónica Nacional de Cuba*) is Cuba's National Symphony Orchestra founded in October, 1959.

On November 11, 1960, the national shymphoniy orchestra realized its first public performance with a concert in the *Teatro Auditórium de La Habana* of that time, now the Teatro Amadeo Roldán. Between national performances and abroad to countries such as Russia, Poland, Yugoslavia, Mexico, Nicaragua, Spain, Peru, Argentina, Martinique and Guadalupe. The orchestra also takes part in record productions and events realized in Cuba, as the international festivals of Guitar, the festival of Contemporary Music, of the New Cine Latinoamericano, and the international festival of ballet of Havana.

Great Theatre of Havana

Great Theatre of Havana	
Type	Theatre
Opened	April 15, 1838
Location	458 Paseo de Prado esquina a San Rafael Havana, Cuba 10600
Owner	City of Havana
Renovated	1914, 2004
Former name(s)	The Great Tacón Theatre Palace of the Galician Centre (Palacio del Centro Gallego)
Capacity	1,500- The Garcia Lorca Hall

The **Great Theatre of Havana** *(Gran Teatro de La Habana)*, was officially opened in 1838 in Havana, Cuba, although its first presentation occurred on November, 1837. Located in Paseo del Prado, in a building known as the *Palacio del Centro Gallego*. Today it is the permanent headquarters of the Cuban National Ballet and the main stage for the International Ballet Festival of Havana. It has rooms of theatres, concert, conferences and video, as well as, galleries of visual, a choral centre, several halls test for danzarias groupings and dancing arts.

History

The building was demolished in 1914 to open the way to the one that currently exists, an exponent in the German neo-baroque architecture style in Havana. The theatre is adorned with a stone and marble statue. There are also sculptural pieces by Giuseppe Moretti, representing allegories depicting benevolence, education, music and theatre. The current building construction began in 1908, was opened in 1915 with an opera season offered by important lyrical figures of the time. It was not until 1985, and as initiative of the prima ballerina Alicia Alonso that the building was renamed and became the Great Theatre of Havana.

The principal theatre is the García Lorca Auditorium, with seats for 1,500 and balconies, it provides a magnificent stage for the Cuban National Ballet Company, as well as other dance and musical performances. During the 19th and 20th century arrived to Cuba to perform in its stage personalities of the highest rank, such as Enrico Caruso, Fanny Elssler, Anna Pavlova, Antonia Mercé, Ruth Saint Denis, Ted Shawn, Vicente Escudero, Maya Plisetskaya, Clorinda Corradi, Sarah Bernhardt, Carla Fracci and Alicia Alonso, as well remarkable companies such as the American Ballet Theatre, the Royal Winnipeg Ballet, Antonio Gades ballet, the Ballet of the Colón Theatre of Buenos Aires, the Ballet Folclórico of Mexico, and many other personalities and ballet companies of high international relief of the 19th and 20th centuries. The theatre also houses the seasons of the *Centre Pro-Art Lírico* with its operas performances, zarzuelas, operettas and concerts, as well as *Spanish Ballet of Havana* and from the Centre of Promotion of the Dance (PRODANZA), it is in addition the International seat of the *Arte Lírico*, the *Practical Courses of the National School of Ballet-CUBALLET*, the Festival *the Track of Spain*, and as well the International Festival of Scenic Oral Narration, and several other festivals.

Gallery

Images of the Great Theatre

Ballet Nacional de Cuba
performing in the Theatre

View from Central Park

References

- El GRAN TEATRO DE LA HABANA es una de las más importantes instituciones culturales de América Latina. [1]
- Radio Habana Cuba Article on The Great Theatre of Havana [2]

External links

- The Great Theatre of Havana at the National Ballet of Cuba homepage [3]

Geographical coordinates: 23°08′13″N 82°21′35″W

National Theater of Cuba

The **National Theater of Cuba** (Spanish: *Teatro Nacional de Cuba*) is a theater in Havana, Cuba, establish September 3, 1979, with a function of gala for the delegations assistants to the VI Summit of the Non-Aligned Movement celebrated in Havana in that year. The theater is housed in a huge modern building, decorated with works by Cuban artists, there are two main theatre stages, the *Avellaneda Hall*(seating for 2254), and the *Covarrubias Hall* (seating for 805), as well as a smaller theatre workshop space on the ninth floor.

National Theater

External links

- National Theater of Cuba homepage [1]

Amadeo Roldán Theater

The **Amadeo Roldán Theater** (Spanish: *Teatro Amadeo Roldán*) is a theater in Havana, Cuba built in 1929. The theater was destroyed in 1977 by a pyromaniac; it was re-open in 1999 as the head office of the National Symphony Orchestra of Cuba which performs seasonal every Sunday at 11:00PM.

Located within a monumental modern building, once home to The Havana Auditorium, the venue now consists of the Amadeo Roldán and García Caturla halls, offering symphonic orchestras, piano recitals, and a mixture of classical and contemporary music. The Amadeo Roldán hall has seats for 886, for important concerts such as Egberto Gismonti and Leo Brouwer, the *Caturla hall* is for small band performances and has a capacity for 276 persons. The theater apart from being home of the National Symphony Orchestra is also home to prestigious international events are held here such as the "Encuentro Internacional de Guitarra" (International Guitar Gathering).

Address

Calzada, e/Calle D y Calle E, Vedado, Havana 10400

References

- *Cuba - Eyewitness Travel Guides* (Dorling Kindersley Publishing, 2004) ISBN 075660172X
- *Havana* (Lonely Planet Publications,2001) ISBN 1864502290
- *The Odyssey Illustrated Guide To Cuba* (Guidebook Company Ltd. , 1995) ISBN 9622173705

Gaia (Havana)

Gaia is an arts centre in Havana, Cuba, set up on January 1, 2000 as a not-for-profit collaboration between Cuban and international artists.[1] [2]

The centre offers theatre, music and dance performances, workshops, programs for children and the physically disadvantaged, and exhibitions of works by young artists. Gaia Teatro, the centre's resident theatre company, has produced some interesting works: *Las cenizas de Ruth* was director Esther Cardoso's radical reinterpretation of the biblical story of Ruth. *Los Reyes* was a staging of Julio Cortázar's version of the tale of Theseus and the Minotaur. And *Reciclaje* used recycled items for wardrobe to explore environmental themes. [3] [4] In collaboration with the British Council, Gaia staged a rehearsed reading of *Cooking with Elvis*, by Lee Hall, directed by British director Sebastian Doggart, in the Teatro Nacional in 2000. Eight years later, on October 4, 2008, the show finally premiered, in the Sala Avellaneda at the Teatro Nacional. [5] [6] It was the first new British play performed in Cuba since *An Inspector Calls* opened in 1947. [2] [7]

Gaia Dance has collaborated with world-renowned Cuban ballerina Viengsay Valdes on a production of *Balance of Ice*, a contemporary dance piece inspired by the sounds of ice sheets calving. The piece was directed by Sebastian Doggart, and featured music by Canadian composer Andrew Staniland. which can be viewed on Youtube. [8]

On the last Saturday of every month, Gaia hosts a mask workshop for children in the morning, and, at 5pm, a unique theatrical event, called *Felices Los Normales (Happy the Normal)*. Targeted at Cubans with HIV/AIDS − and the community surrounding them -- the program is directed by inspirational activist Carlos Borbon. He and his group, Teatro Espontaneo, invite participants to come forward to tell an HIV-related story which is then enacted by a group of professional actors and musicians. The stories are moving and dramatic, and the atmosphere is electric. In December 2006, UNESCO presented the company with an award for its efforts in combating HIV/AIDS. [9]

Gaia also has a 'Casa de Mascara', teaching the techniques and traditions of masks to children and adults, and taking promenade performances into the streets of Old Havana.

Gaia has hosted numerous exhibitions of Cuban and international artists, including Leysis Quesada Vera, Angel Delgado, Catherine Bertola, Paul Rooney and US artist Scott Griesbach. [10]. In 2006, it put on an exhibition -- *Kachita, Mango y el Jim* -- startlingly documenting the havoc caused by two hurricanes that flooded the city in 2005.

Gaia has staged performances by musicians such as Chucho Valdes, [11] Tony Perez, Los Jovenes Clasicos del Son, Sonora Matancera, Alicia Bustamante, Gaia Jazz, and Aris Garit.[12] It offers percussion lessons for foreign music students.

Gaia Teatro is located at Calle Brazil (Teniente Rey) #157, between Cuba y Aguiar, La Habana Vieja.[1] In 2007, Gaia embarked on major construction work to create permanent workshops for its arts and community activities, including the building of a new semi-outdoors performance space.

References

- *Time Out: Havana*, Penguin Books, 2001, ISBN 0-14-100029-5
- *Time Out: Havana*, Time Out Guides, 2005, ISBN 1904978-83-5
- *Time Out: Havana*, Time Out Guides, 2007

Hubert de Blanck Theater

The **Hubert de Blanck Theater** is a small theatre situated on *Calle Calzada* in the Vedado district of Havana, Cuba, named after Hubert de Blanck. It has a seating capacity for 267 people, and offers regular performances of contemporary and classical plays. There are also occasional presentations of well-known foreign productions that have toured to Cuba.

Address

Calle Calzada, No. 654 entre A y B,
Vedado, Havana, 10400

Karl Marx Theater

The **Karl Marx Theater** (Spanish: *Teatro Karl Marx*) is a theater in Havana, Cuba, formerly known as the *Teatro Blanquita*, and renamed after the Cuban Revolution of 1959, the venue has an enormous auditorium with seating capacity of 5500 people, and is generally used for big shows by stars from Cuba and abroad. The theatre is also a major concert venue for both local and international artists; singer-songwriters such as Carlos Varela, Silvio Rodríguez and Pablo Milanés, are just a few of the great names who have graced this particular stage. More recently, this was the scene of a concert by the band Manic Street Preachers, which included among the thousands of excited young fans none other than President Fidel Castro himself. On being warned by the band that they would be playing very loud, he retorted "you cannot be louder than war!".

Address

Ave 1ª, entre 8 y 10,
Miramar, Playa, Havana,
11300

International Ballet Festival of Havana

The **International Ballet Festival of Havana** *(Festival de Ballet de La Habana)*, is a ballet festival held in the Great Theater of Havana, Cuba every two years. Created in 1960 by a joint effort of the Ballet Nacional de Cuba, the *Instituto Nacional de la Industria Turística* and the cultural organizations of the government, the International Ballet Festival of Havana was added to the plans of massive diffusion of arts started after the popular Cuban revolution on January 1, 1959. The Festival, with its character, has allowed people to enjoy the performances and the works of prestigious figures of the world

Great Theater of Havana opera house. Home of the International Festivals

of the dance and has also shown to the visitors the high level reached by the Cuban ballet. In the year 2000 it celebrated its 42nd anniversary. This defines it as one of the oldest of all held in the world. Created in 1960 it quickly became one of the most transcendental events of the national Cuban culture and of the international dance as well.

Festivals

1st through 6th festivals

The years that followed the first three festivals, 1960, 1966 and 1967, were a long and fruitful work period recorded as one of the most beautiful pages in the history of the Ballet Nacional de Cuba since its casting was enriched with the first graduates from the *Escuela Nacional de Ballet* (National Ballet School), its consolidation as one of the dance companies of greatest international prestige and the heroic battles fought against the unfair barrier that didn't allow its worldwide recognition. The 4th Festival was held in 1974 and was dedicated to the 2nd Congress of the *Federación de Mujeres Cubanas* and from that year on the festival was celebrated every two years and has emphasized this peculiar aspect that has characterized its work. The 5th Festival was dedicated to the 30th Anniversary of the Granma landing. The 6th festival was dedicated to the 30th anniversary of the Foundation of the Ballet Nacional de Cuba and to the 35th anniversary of Alicia Alonso's debut in the role of Giselle. This festival also made an emphasis on "the premiere of works created for the company by well-known international choreographers, Cuban and foreign".

7th & 8th festivals

The 7th festival was dedicated to highlight the *relationship of ballet with the rest of the arts* and in it together with the *Premiere Nights, Repertoire Nights* with the usual works of the BNC and the *Concerts of International Stars*, there were galas dedicated to the dramatic theater, the plastic arts, the music, the cinema, the folklore and the literature as well as special galas dedicated to the birthday of the great Russian choreographer Mikhail Fokin and to the ballet Giselle on occasion of the performance of the couple made up by the Prima Ballerina Assoluta Alicia Alonso and the famous Russian dancer Vladimir Vasiliev. The 8th festival gave special attention to *The presence of Latin America in its choreographic creation* allowed knowing roots, experiences, ways and achievements of the dance in the continent. A transcendental event was the beginning, parallel to the festival, of the First International Practical Course of the Cuban School of Ballet, that was attended by dancers, advanced students and observers from eleven American and European countries as well as a big Cuban representation that created a tradition that stands up to now.

9th festival and 10th

The 9t. Festival put an emphasis on *The styles and the choreographers*, this made possible to see a panoramic of the principal choreographic landmarks that ballet has known throughout its history. The 10th celebration was a great opportunity for the festival to be a great party of art and friendship with the presence of hundreds of guests among them famous stars and dance companies coming from all over the world who, together with the members of the Ballet Nacional de Cuba and other groups, carried out a varied program.

11th through 14th

The llth. Festival was dedicated to two important anniversaries: the 150th anniversary of the Gran Teatro de La Habana, the oldest theatrical institution of the country and the 40th anniversary of the foundation of the Ballet Nacional de Cuba. The 12th. Had a slogan: *Past, present and choreographic future* and showed a rich sample of styles and tendencies present in the dance of our times. Festival 13th emphasized in *The Iberian American presence in the art of ballet* while it commemorated the 5th Centennial of the Encounter of the American and European Cultures and faithful to this credo participated in the festival important companies, stars and personalities of the dance in Spain and Iberian America that offered a rich sample arisen from the talent and common zeal of these cultural aspects. The 14th. Festival pointed out *The diversity and richness of the choreographic art* with an attractive offer of styles and tendencies within the academic, contemporary and folkloric dance and where galas dedicated to Romanticism and Classicism excelled as well as concert programs with Cuban and foreign artists and the performances of nearly a dozen guest companies.

15th festival

The 15th Festival emphasized on *The composers or musical styles that had the greatest influence in dance*. There were galas dedicated to Cuban and French composers, to baroque composers, to Frédéric Chopin, Igor Stravinski and Manuel de Falla- to commemorate the 120th anniversary of his birthday and the 50th of his death-, and as well to the Russian composer Pyotr Ilyich Tchaikovsky, key figure in the classic ballet.

16th festival

The 16th Festival was dedicated to a transcendental anniversary: the *50th Anniversary of the foundation of the Ballet Nacional de Cuba*. Hundreds of guests were present on this occasion among them companies such as Julio Bocca's from Argentina, the *Ballet of Zaragoza*, the Spanish Ballet of Murcia (Spain), the *Soloist Group from the Komische Opera of Berlin* and the *Great Dessau Theater* (Germany) the *Diastases Group* (Cyprus), the Company dance Theater of Turin (Italy); Introdans *Ensemble Voor der Jeugd* (The Netherlands) as well as *Kennedy's Tap Dance Company* and The *Alvin Ailey Repertory Ensemble*, both from the United States. The guest list was made up by the famous

Italian ballerina Carla Fracci, who came to give prestige to this event after 24 years of her first visit in 1974, as well as stars belonging to well-known companies such as the Paris Opera Ballet, the Ballet of the Teatro alla Scala from Milan, the American Ballet Theatre, the New York City Ballet, the Bolshoi Ballet of Moscow, the Ballet Estable of the Colon Theater from Argentina, the Royal Danish Ballet, the Ballet of the Opera of Berlin, the National Hungarian Ballet, the Classical Ballet of Guangzhou, China, the Ballet of the Municipal Theater of Rio de Janeiro, and the National Dance Company of Mexico, among others. Collateral activities such as the presentation of the book Ballet Nacional de Cuba: *Half a Century of Glory*, written by the historian Miguel Cabrera, a stamp cancellation, photographic and plastic arts and movie and video exhibitions were part of the festival. Two important moments in this festival were the inauguration of the Dance Museum and the celebration of the 1st Iberian American Choreographic Competition organized by the General Society of Authors and Editors (SGAE), the Author's Foundation and the Ballet Nacional de Cuba.

17th & 18th festival

The 17th Festival was dedicated to highlight *the principal creators and choreographic tendencies that have enriched ballet in the 20th century* and in it were present besides the Cubans, six foreign companies among them the Ballet of Washington, the folkloric Ballet of Puebla, The *Da Capo company and the Dance Group* (Azahar) from Valencia, Spain. There were also other representatives from seventeen countries of America, Asia and Australia. The 18th festival was inaugurated by Fidel Castro, President of the State and Ministers Council of Cuba and the festival slogan was *Past, present and future of the dance*. Four foreign companies among them the Dessau Ballett from Germany, and the choreographic Center of Valencia, Spain were present as well as seven Cuban companies and dancers, choreographers and special guests coming from fifteen countries of America, Europe and Asia. During the event it was announced the winning work of the 3rd Iberian American Choreographic Competition that corresponded to the Cuban George Enrique Céspedes' work *Por favor, no me limites...*, and a wide repertoire that performed in galas and concerts showed the representative works of the most valuable romantic-classical inheritance of the 19th century, as well as contemporary creations of Cuban and foreign choreographers. A wide group of collateral activities that included plastic arts, photographic and movie exhibitions and conferences, enriched the festival.

Beyond

After more than four decades of work, the International Ballet Festival of Havana goes forward keeping its creative potentiality in the promisory future of the 21st century.

Throughout its more than four decades of productive existence, possible thanks to the agglutinative gift of Alicia Alonso and the unmovable support of the cultural organizations of the Cuban state, the International Ballet Festival of Havana has wished and known how to be a meeting of the best of art endowed with a typical feature that at the same time that singles it out, contributes to strengthen its well earned prestige. Enough to say that in these forty-two years of existence, fifty-eight foreign companies have been present and about a thousand guests (dancers, choreographers, pedagogues, designers, soloists, composers, critics and observers) coming from fifty-two countries of the five continents. The known encouragement offered to the creation not only of Cuban choreographers but foreign ones as well representatives of the most valuable and different tendencies of the contemporary art of the dance, has made possible the premiere of 777 works, 198 of them were world premieres and 579 were premieres in Cuba. Its multiple collateral activities (photographic and plastic arts, cinema exhibitions, philatelic and poster editions as well as editions of specialized books, among others).

Participated countries in the Ballet Festivals

- Americas (19)

Argentina, Brazil, Canada, Colombia, Costa Rica, Chile, Ecuador, United States, Guatemala, French Guyana, Martinique, Mexico, Nicaragua, Panama, Peru, Puerto Rico, Dominican Republic, Uruguay, Venezuela.

- Europe (26)

Austria, Belgium, Bulgaria, former Czechoslovakia, Cyprus, Denmark, Spain, Russian Federation, Finland, France, Great Britain, Greece, Holland, Hungary, Italy, Latvia, Norway, Poland, Portugal, former German Democratic Republic, former German Federal Republic, Romania, Sweden, Switzerland, former Soviet Union and Yugoslavia.

- Asia (6)

Philippines, Japan, Vietnam, People's Republic of China, Israel and Kazakhstan

- Africa (4)

Angola, Algeria, Egypt, Guinea.

- Oceania (1)

Australia.

Total: 56 countries

Choreographic Premieres

World premieres: 198

Premieres in Cuba: 579

Total: 777 premieres

See also

- Aspendos International Opera and Ballet Festival
- Canadian Ballet Festival
- USA International Ballet Competition

External links

- International Ballet of Havana at the National Ballet of Cuba homepage [3]

Havana Film Festival

The **Havana Film Festival** is a Cuban festival that focuses on the promotion of Spanish-language filmmakers. It is also known in Spanish as *Festival Internacional del Nuevo Cine Latinoamericano de La Habana*, and in English as Festival of New Latinamerican Cinema of La Havana.

The festival takes place every year during December in the city of Havana, Cuba.

The festival first began in December 3, 1979. The president of the first organizing committee was Alfredo Guevara and more than 600 film directors of Latin America responded to the first call made by the Cuban Institute of the Cinematographic Art and Industry (ICAIC).

Awards

Within the following categories, approximately 40 awards are given:

- Films
- Documentaries
- Animation
- First Work
- Direction
- Cinematography
- Other Awards, including a FIPRESCI prize

Grand Coral - First Prize (partial)

- 2009: *La teta asustada* (2009) -- (Perú and Spain)
- 2008: *Tony Manero* (2008) -- (Chile and Brazil)
- 2007: *Stellet Licht* (2007) -- (Mexico)
- 2006: *O Céu de Suely* (2006) -- (Brazil)
- 2005: *Iluminados por el fuego* (2005) -- (Argentina)
- 2004: *Whisky* (2004) -- (Uruguay)
- 2003: *Suite Habana* (2003) -- (Cuba, documentary)
- 2002: *City of God* (2002) -- (Brazil)
- 2002: *Tan de repente* (2002)
- 2001: *La Ciénaga* (2001) -- (Argentina)
- 2000: *Me You Them* (2000)
- 1999: *Garage Olimpo* (1999)(Argentina)
- 1998: *La vida es silbar* (1998)(Cuba)
- 1997: *Martín (Hache)* (1997) -- (Argentina and Spain)
- 1996: *Profundo carmesí* (1996)
- 1995: *El callejón de los milagros* (1995)
- 1994: *Principio y fin* (1993)
- 1986: *A Hora da Estrela* (1985) -- (Brazil)

External links

- Havana Film Festival [1] official website (Spanish).

Havana's International Book Fair

Havana's International Book Fair (Spanish: "Feria Internacional del Libro de La Habana) is an annual public festival to promote books and writing that spans between February and March. The festival begins in Havana at the Fortaleza de San Carlos de la Cabaña, an 18th century Spanish construction, and spreads east and west of the capital to all provinces and many municipalities. The book fair ends in the eastern city of Santiago de Cuba. The fair first took place in 1982, and occurred every two years until 2000 when it became an annual tradition. The festival consists of book vendors, poetry readings, children's activities, art exhibitions, and concerts in the evenings. It is considered Cuba's premier cultural event, as well as the event with the highest attendance in Havana. The 18th annual International Book Fair in 2009 had approximately 600,000 visitors. Literacy in Cuba is one of the greatest legacies of the Cuban Revolution of 1959. The law that established the National Press of Cuba was one of the first measures of the revolution. In 1961, Cuba launched a National Literacy Campaign and today, according to the United Nations, Cuba has the highest literacy rate in the world. Along with the public, the book fair is attended by Cuban and international authors, publishers, and political officials. Over 100 publishing houses present catalogues of books, including Casa de las Américas. Each book fair is dedicated to a genre, issue, or author, and also a guest of honor. Since 2000, each book fair has been dedicated to Cuban authors and intellectuals.

Snapshots from XVI International Book Fair at Morro-Cabaña

External links

- Book Fair Enthralls Havana [1] *Havana Times*, Feb 14, 2009
- Trotsky in Havana [2] by Dmitri Prieto, *Havana Times*, March 26, 2009

Havana biennial

The **Havana Biennial Art Exhibition** takes place in Havana (Cuba) every two years, and principally aims at promoting the **« Third World » contemporary art**. The biennial is considered as an important forum for underrepresented voices, and Latin American and Caribbean artists still have priority even though artists from all over the world are authorised to submit their works.

Since its first edition in 1984, the Biennial event has had central themes, among them tradition and contemporary times, challenges, art, society and reflection, man and his memory, life with art and urban life. The works submitted by the artists include mainly paintings and two-dimensional work, using a wide variety of techniques and trends.

History

The first Havana Biennial was established in 1984, long before the worldwide boom of biennials that emerged in the mid-nineties. This first edition of the festival focused on artists from Latin America and the Caribbean only.

Since the second Havana Biennial in 1986, the focus extended to include art from Africa and Asia, thus becoming the most important meeting place for artists from "non-Western" countries.

The Havana Biennial has not always been able to take place on during the two-year rotation due to funding challenges. The 8th Biennial of 2002 did was delayed an entire year, resuming in November 2003. This Biennial was however noteworthy as it showcased art functioning within the social landscape, outside of traditional institutions. By bringing art out the museum and into the streets, artists that would normally be unable to participate within large institutions, or who prefer to work outside of such institutions are able to better engage diverse audiences. Noteworthy artists to have "activated" the urban space include Mitchell Sipus and Fabiana De Barros.

At the beginning, the first two Biennial events included an awards ceremony, but then the organizing committee decided to make it a non-competitive event.

10th Havana Biennial - 25th Anniversary

With a central theme called "Integration and resistance in the Globalization Era", the 10th Havana Biennial Art Exhibition took place from March 27 to April 30, 2009. Experts from the Wifredo Lam Contemporary Art Center reviewed more than 400 proposals submitted by artists from 44 nations. For the first time, the organisers decided to include in the Biennial western countries.

In addition to fine arts exhibitions, the 10th Havana Biennial also included conferences, workshops and master classes, documentaries and video screenings. The artists transformed the city into a showcase of contemporary art, taking over all the available urban spaces and municipal galleries.

Topics which have piqued the interest of artists this year include the tensions between tradition and contemporary reality, challenges to the historical processes of colonization, the relationships between art and society, individuals and memory, the effects of technological development on human communication and the dynamics of urban culture.

The group of curators for this 2009 Biennial was made up by Margarita González, Nelson Herrera Ysla, José Manuel Noceda, Ibis Hernández Abascal, Margarita Sánchez Prieto, José Fernández Portal and Dannys Montes de Oca Moreda.

Selection of Cuban Artists Projects :

- JEFF – « Herd of elephants »
- Mario M. González – Collective exhibition on the global theme "Flag" with around 200 artists
- Wilfredo Prieto – « Star in the sky of Havana »
- Liset Castillo – « Archaeology of power »
- Yoan Capote – « Open Mind »
- René Francisco Rodriguez – « Interpret »
- Alexander Beatón – « The Permanent Race »
- Duvier Del Dago – « The Black Box »
- Los Carpentiros – « Fluido »

Further reading

- Rojas-Sotelo, Miguel Leonardo. "Cultural Maps, Networks, and Flows: The History and Impact of the Havana Biennale 1984 to the present [1]." Dissertation, University of Pittsburgh, 2009.

External links

- The 10th Havana Biennial on video [2]
- Havana Biennial [3] Official Website
- Havana Biennial [4] Overview by the Miami Herald
- Havana Biennial [5] Article by the New York Times
- Exclusive Pictures of the Havana Biennial 2009 [6]

Malecón, Havana

The **Malecón** is a broad esplanade, roadway and seawall which stretches for 8 km along the coast in Havana, Cuba, from the mouth of Havana Harbor in Old Havana to Vedado.

Construction of the Malecón began in 1901, during temporary U.S. military rule. It was completed in three stages

- in 1901 and 1902, from the Paseo del Prado to Calle Crespo
- between 1902 and 1921 as far as the Monument to the Maine
- between 1948 and 1952 to the mouth of the Almendares River

There are a number of important monuments along the Malecón, including those to General Máximo Gomez, Antonio Maceo and General Calixto García.

Significant buildings include the Castillo de la Real Fuerza, the Castillo de San Salvador de la Punta, the Torreón de San Lázaro, the Hotel Nacional and the United States Interests Section in Havana.

External links

- Guije.com (in Spanish) [1]
- Pictures from Google [2]

Geographical coordinates: 23°8′30″N 82°22′05″W

Manzana de Gomez

Manzana de Gomez (*Gomez' Block*), a 20th century building in Havana, was the first shopping mall in Cuba. It is 5 stories tall. It was built by Jose Gomez Mena. The 1910 landmark structure was the first European-style shopping arcade in Cuba.

The Manzana de Gomez, was the first entire city block built in Cuba in the beginnings of the 20th century completely for commercial use with two inner diagonal streets that cross the building in all directions integrating the pedestrian circulation with the outer fabric. It is bounded by the streets of Neptuno, San Rafael, Zulueta and Monserrate.

Manzana de Gomez

References

- *Cuba - Eyewitness Travel Guides* (Dorling Kindersley Publishing, 2004) ISBN 075660172X
- *Havana* (Lonely Planet Publications,2001) ISBN 1864502290
- *The Odyssey Illustrated Guide To Cuba* (Guidebook Company Ltd. , 1995) ISBN 9622173705

Geographical coordinates: 23°08′16.86″N 82°21′28.54″W

Attractions

Santa María del Mar, Cuba

This article is about the beach in Havana, Cuba. For other uses, see Santa María del Mar (disambiguation)

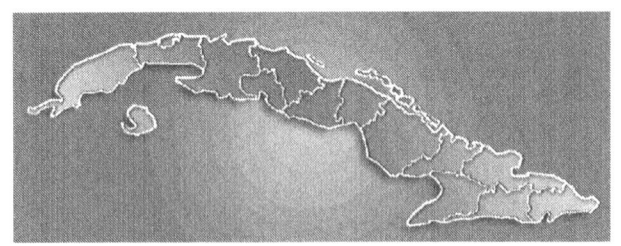

Location of Santa María del Mar in Cuba

Santa María del Mar is a sandy beach located 12 miles east of Havana, Cuba along the Via Blanca highway.

It is a segment of a chain of beaches called the Eastern Beaches Spanish: *Playas del Este* which extend for 15 miles along the north coast of Havana province in the municipality of Habana del Este.

Geographical coordinates: 23°10′21″N 82°11′30″W

Tarara

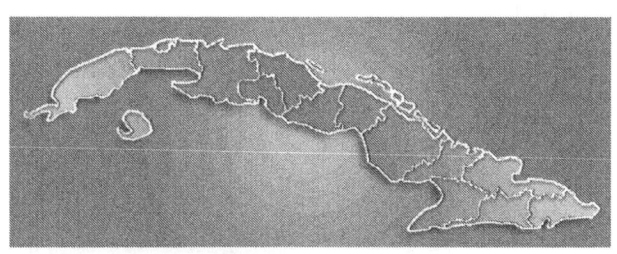

Location of Tarara in Cuba

Tarara (Spanish: *Tarará*) is a gated resort town in the municipality of Habana del Este in the city of Havana, Cuba. It is about 19km east of the city centre and west of other beaches including Santa Maria del Mar and Guanabo.

Geography

This resort community was built in the 1940s in Art Deco style on a hill facing the Atlantic Ocean. A small marina is located in an inlet west of the town. An amusement park was located across from this inlet, but now (2006) lies in ruins. While there's hardly any evidence of its past existence on the ground, the aerial view reveals a pentagram shape .The Pentagram does not belong to Playa Tarara, but to Playa Celimar. It was built after 1959 as an amusement park for "Pioneros of Cuba" organization.

History

Tarara was developed in the 1940's by American Royal S. Webster as a complete town, with residences, stores, a movie theatre, a marina, a public park and beach facilities. Many considered the Tarara beach to be one of the most beautiful on the island, with its boardwalk a popular weekend destination. Tarara was a fast and easy trip to Havana and the airport, with newly paved highways going directly to the resort. Mr. Webster lived there as well, as did many of his children.

After the Cuban Revolution, in January of 1959, Che Guevara went to live at a summer villa in Tarara to recover from a violent asthma attack. While there he started the Tarara Group, a group that debated and formed the new plans for Cuba's social, political, and economic development. In addition, Che began to write his book Guerrilla Warfare while resting at Tarara. Che returned to Tarara in June of 1959 for his honeymoon after his marriage to his second wife Aleida March.

Beach in Tarara

At the height of tight Cuban-Soviet relations, the town housed Russian officials stationed in Cuba, and for a while (early 1990's) functioned as a recovery resort for Ukrainian children affected by the Chernobyl nuclear disaster . After 2000 (and the partial opening of Cuba to foreign investments), this was a place of choice for foreign companies representatives that were doing business in Cuba, with the residences functioning as rental villas.

In 2005, the town was turned into a recovery resort for blind patients from Venezuela, part of a deal between Fidel Castro and Hugo Chávez, in which Cuba offered medical expertise in return for Venezuelean oil .

In 2007, the town began to receive Chinese students, especially high school graduates. This is under a project in which the Cuban government provides scholarships and facilities for those Chinese to learn Spanish.

The Tarara beach houses can now be leased for a minimum one year from the government for foreign and embassy employees. In previous years Canadians, Italians and Spanish visitors rented the beach houses for long stay vacations for 1-6 months, but this has not been re-established yet as of 2009. Many houses have been renovated recently again due to interior destruction from the Venezuelan people's misuse. The Cuban doctors now go to Venezuela to treat eye patients.

Oil discovery

In 2006, oil was discovered in a well near Tarara.

Sources

- Castaneda, Jorge, *The Life and Death of Che Guevara: Companero*, New York: Vintage Books (1998) ISBN 0-679-75940-9

Geographical coordinates: 23°10′37″N 82°12′14″W

John Lennon Park

John Lennon Park or **Parque John Lennon** is a public park, located in the Vedado district in Havana, Cuba.

On one of the benches of the park, nearer the corner of streets 17th and 6th, there is a sculpture of the former Beatles member John Lennon, sculpted by Cuban artist José Villa Soberón, seated on the bench's right half. On a marble tile at the foot of the bench there is an inscription reading: "Dirás que soy un soñador pero no soy el único" *John Lennon*, which is a Spanish translation of the English lyrics, "You may say I'm a dreamer, but I'm not the only one," from the song "Imagine".

The sculpture of Lennon is currently not wearing his signature round-lens glasses, which have been stolen, or vandalized, several times. However, during the day, an old security guard can be found sitting next to the bench, and he will place glasses on the statue if there is a request.

The statue was unveiled on 8th December 2000, by President Fidel Castro. One year later, Cuban author Ernesto Juan Castellanos wrote a book about the statue, John Lennon en La Habana with a little help from my friends, and about the ban that John Lennon and The Beatles suffered in Cuba during the '1960s and '1970s.

Gallery

References

CNN article [1]

Geographical coordinates: 23°07′55″N 82°24′01″W

Bodeguita del medio

Geographical coordinates: 23°08′27″N 82°21′08″W

La Bodeguita del Medio is a typical restaurant-bar of Havana (Cuba). It is very famous[citation needed] and touristy for the personalities that have patronized it: Salvador Allende, the poet Pablo Neruda, the writer Ernest Hemingway and many others. La Bodeguita is also known as the birthplace of the Mojito cocktail, prepared in the bar since its opening in 1942.

The rooms full of curious objects, frames, photos, as well as the walls covered by signatures of famous or unknown customers, recount the island's past. Along with the local food, cigars, music and mojitos, la Bodeguita del Medio offers a glimpse of Cuba's typical atmosphere.

Outside view of Bodeguita del Medio

History

In 1942, Angel Martinez bought out the small *Bodega La Complaciente* in Empedrado Street, in the old Havana district. He renamed the place Casa Martinez. Angel Martinez sold typical Cuban products and, from time to time, served dinner to the regulars. But mainly, the people who were found at the Casa Martinez, were there to have a drink with their friends, and savor a brand new cocktail called Mojito, made with rum, mint, sugar, lemon and club soda.

Inside view of Bodeguita del Medio

In 1949, the cook Silvia Torres aka "la china" prepared the food. Very quickly, the Casa Martinez became the centre of Havana's cultural effervescence. Attracted by the bohemian charm of the place, writers, choreographers, musicians or journalists met there in a convivial ambiance. Encouraged by a the need for restaurants in the Old Havana at the end of the 50s, the place started to serve food to everyone.

In April 26, 1950, the name Bodeguita del Medio was officially adopted.

Name's origin

Among the first clients was Felito Ayon, a charismatic editor, who rubbed shoulders with the avant-garde of Havana, and put Casa Martinez on the map amongst his acquaintances. It is the way Felito Ayon used to indicate the location of the Bodeguita to his friends, that made popular the expression **Bodeguita del Medio**, that was to become its official name in 1950.

Menu

The menu is typically Creole: boiled rice, black beans, pork shank, manioc, pig shank roasted in its juice, pork rinds and toasted fried plantains.

Regulars

Numerous artists and celebrities were regulars of the Bodeguita : the poet Pablo Neruda, Gabriel Garcia Marquez, Gabriela Mistral, Agustín Lara, Nat King Cole, Marlene

Hemingway handwriting in La Bodeguita del Medio

Dietrich, Nicolás Guillén and Ernest Hemingway. "My mojito in La Bodeguita, My daiquiri in El Floridita" can still be read on the wall today, in Hemingway´s handwriting.[1]

La Bodeguita worldwide

Today, there are establishments of the restaurant in other places of the world such as Mexico, United-States, Ukraine, Czech Republic, Macedonia, Slovakia, Colombia, Venezuela, Germany, England and Argentina. In Spain, a company has opened four Bodeguitas del Medio, perfect replicas of the original Cuban restaurant. Today, tourists and locals continue to go to La Bodeguita del Medio to drink the authentic Cuban mojito

External links

- labodeguitadelmedio.com.mx [2], Site of La Bodeguita del Medio Mexican restaurants chain
- tripadvisor.com [3], La Bodeguita del Medio
- bodeguita.com.ua [4], La Bodeguita del Medio in Kyiv, Ukraine
- havana-guide.com [5]
- youtube.com [6], *Hasta siempre Commandante* performed in Bodeguita del Medio
- fotopedia.com [7], Selected photos of Bodeguita del medio

Floridita

Geographical coordinates: 23°08′14″N 82°21′26″W

Floridita or **El Floridita** is an historic restaurant and bar in the older part of Havana (*La Habana Vieja*), Cuba. It lies at the end of *Calle Obispo* (Bishop Street), across Monserrate Street from the **The National Museum of Fine Arts of Havana** (*Museo Nacional de Bellas Artes de La Habana*). The establishment is famous for its daiquiris and for having being one of the favourite hangouts of Ernest Hemingway in Havana.

El Floridita bar. The bar "patron" at center, below the wall-mounted photo, is a life-sized bronze statue of Ernest Hemingway

" My mojito in *La Bodeguita*, my daiquiri in *El Floridita* "

—Ernest Hemingway

History

It opened in 1817 with the name "La Piña de Plata" (English: *The Silver Pineapple*) in the place it still occupies, in the corner of Obispo and Monserrate streets. Almost 100 years later, the large number of North American tourists persuaded the owner to change the name to "El Florida", but with time it became popularly known as "El Floridita".

Ernest and Mary Hemingway with Spencer Tracy at the bar corner in *El Floridita*, Havana, Cuba, ca. 1955. The window behind Hemingway is the one showing in the modern photo above.

In 1914, the Catalan immigrant Constantino Ribalaigua Vert started working in the bar as *cantinero* (bartender). Constantino, nicknamed *Constante*, became the owner in 1918. Constante is credited for inventing the frozen daiquiri in the early 1930s, a drink that became linked to the fame of the place, whose motto is now "la cuna del daiquiri" (the cradle of the daiquiri). The bar became a school of highly skilled *cantineros* (bartenders) specialised in cocktails prepared with fresh fruit juices and rum, whose traditions are still preserved by the disciples of Constante.

The Nobel Prize-winning American writer Ernest Hemingway frequented the bar, which is at the end of *Calle Obispo* (Bishop Street), a short walk from the Hotel Ambos Mundos where Hemingway maintained a room from 1932-1939. Hemingway's children also noted that in the early 1940s Hemingway and his wife "Marty" (Martha Gellhorn) continued to drive from their house outside Havana (Finca Vigía) to the Floridita, for drinks. The establishment today contains many noticeable memorabilia of the author, with photographs, a bust and, more recently (2003), a life-size bronze statue at   the   end

2003 statue of Ernest Hemingway by José Villa Soberón inside *El Floridita* bar, at the wall end of the bar (see photo at beginning of article). A photograph of Hemingway awarding Fidel Castro a prize in a fishing contest in May, 1960 (almost a year and a half after the Cuban revolution) adorns the wall behind the statue.

of the bar near the wall, sculpted by the Cuban artist José Villa Soberón.

Hemingway wasn't the only famous customer of the bar. The establishment was frequented by many generations of Cuban and foreign intellectuals and artists. Graham Greene, the British novelist who wrote Our Man in Havana was also a frequent customer during his stay in Cuba as diplomat and spy.

The place still preserves much of the atmosphere of the 1940s and 1950s, with the red coats of the bartenders matching the Regency style decoration that dates from the 1950s, although now most of its customers are occasional tourists. Besides the cocktails, the place is reputed for the (expensive) sea food.

The restaurant of *El Floridita*

External links

- "El Floridita" [1]. *World's Best Bars*. Retrieved 2009-12-12.

- "El Floridita" [2]. *Frommer's*. Retrieved 2009-12-12.

- Hernández, Reina (2007-04-10). "The Most Famous Patron of the Most Famous Bar in Havana" [3]. *CubaNow.net*. Retrieved 2009-12-12.

Tropicana Club

Tropicana is a world known cabaret and club in Havana, Cuba. It was launched in 1939 at Villa Mina, a six-acre (24,000 m²) suburban estate with lush tropical gardens in Havana's Marianao neighborhood.

Influence

The Tropicana had an impact in spreading Cuban culture internationally. New York's Tropicana was a Latin music club launched in

Club Tropicana Dancers

1945 by two Cuban restaurateurs, the brothers Manolo and Tony Alfaro, who made it the most glamorous nightclub in the Bronx. On the TV series *I Love Lucy*, the character Ricky Ricardo (played by Cuban-born Desi Arnaz) was a singer and bandleader at Manhattan's fictional Tropicana nightclub, now recreated in reality in Jamestown, New York at the Lucille Ball-Desi Arnaz Center's Tropicana Room. In 2004, the Atlantic City Tropicana opened The Quarter, which attempts to recreate the architecture, atmosphere and cuisine of Old Havana during the 1940s. In its September 1956 issue, *Show* magazine displayed a four-page spread on *Tropicana* (1957), a Mexican musical comedy filmed on location at the cabaret and featuring some of the Tropicana's performers.

History

The spectacular showplace that became The Tropicana evolved out of a Depression-era bohemian nightclub called Edén Concert, operated by Cuban impresario Victor de Correa. One day, two casino operators approached de Correa about opening a combination casino and cabaret on property on the outskirts of Havana rented from Guillermina Pérez Chaumont, known as Mina. The operators felt that the tropical gardens of her Villa Mina, would provide a lush natural setting for an outdoor cabaret. They cut a deal, and in December 1939, de Correa moved his company of singers, dancers and musicians into a converted mansion located on the estate. De Correa provided the food and entertainment, while Rafael Mascaro and Luis Bular operated the casino located in the chandeliered dining room of the estate's mansion. Originally known as El Beau Site, de Correa decided to rename the club Tropicana, because of its tropical atmosphere and "na" after the last syllable of the original owner, Mina. With a fanfare from the Alfredo Brito Orchestra, the Club Tropicana, opened on

December 30, 1939. Its popularity with tourists grew steadily until the outbreak of World War II, which sharply curtailed tourism to Cuba.

During this time, Martín Fox, a burly, gregarious and well-connected gambler, began renting table space in the casino. Eventually, by 1950, he would amass enough profits to take over the lease of what would become The Tropicana. Martin Fox came to Havana from the countryside. They nicknamed "Guajiro Fox" (Fox, the peasant or country bumpkin) and he was big in the numbers of racket. As a person born and raised in the country, he loved plants and become their most ardent keeper. He had no education whatsoever, but he was bold and has close relations with the more solvent groups. Thus, in a few years he toppled Victor de Correa and, together with Alberto Ardura and Oscar Echemendia, formed an entrepreneurial trilogy that made Tropicana one of the most famous nightclubs in the continent. Hanging in through tough times, which included a temporary ban on casino gambling, Fox bought out de Correa's interest in 1951 and tapped Alberto Ardura and Oscar Echemendia to replace him. This is when Tropicana's glory years really began. Ardura hired maverick choreographer Roderico "Rodney" Neyra away from his chief rival on the cabaret scene, the Club San Souci, and Fox contracted up-and-coming Max Borges-Recio, who created Tropicana's Arcos de Cristal, parabolic concrete arches and glass walls over an indoor stage. Construction continued through 1951. Giant fruit trees were left in situ during construction to punctuate the interior. When the indoor cabaret at the air-conditioned Arcos de Cristal opened on March 15, 1952, it had a combined total seating capacity of 1,700 for the interior and outside areas with furniture designed by Charles Eames. The Arcos de Cristal won numerous international prizes when it was built and was one of only six Cuban buildings included in the landmark 1954 Museum of Modern Art exhibit entitled "Latin American Architecture since 1945."

But it was the arrival in Havana in 1946 of Floridian mobster Santo "Louie Santos" Trafficante Jr. that would alter the future of The Tropicana. Trafficante, Jr. had been sent by his father, Tampa godfather Santo Trafficante, Sr. (a man who always wanted to make it big in Cuba) to oversee La Cosa Nostra and Tampa Family casino and business interests there. Upon Trafficante, Sr.'s death in 1954, Santo, Jr. succeeded his father as boss of Tampa. That same year, as Trafficante, Jr.'s control of Tampa's lucrative bolita racket had been threatened by congressional hearings on mob activities in the U.S., he officially settled in Havana along with Meyer Lansky. Lansky would become the top syndicate figure in Cuba, appointing Trafficante his second in command.

Within a few years, Trafficante owned or held stakes in both The Tropicana and The Sans Souci (the only casinos which been operating in Havana for several years prior to 1955). Both clubs served drinks and meals which just about covered the operating costs. The profits from gambling amounted to approximately $5,000 a day, after "deductions". It was suspected that he also had behind-the-scenes interests in other syndicate owned Cuban gambling casinos namely those at, The Habana Riviera, The Nacional, The Sevilla-Biltmore, The Capri and the Havana Hilton. The newer casinos averaged even higher profits while the profits of the two original casinos remained more or less the same. Ironically,

Lansky and Trafficante both avoided gambling. "Bartenders don't drink, because they see the consequences," Trafficante said at one point. "I know the odds are stacked against the players." According to a 1958 Treasury Department investigation The Tropicana casino (along with those at The Capri and The Nacional) were rumored to be using "bust-out dice" and "rigged equipment." According to their information the slot machines were "rigged for a very low pay off, due to the extremely high take off of the proceeds by officials."

Even though he retained Martín Fox and his brother Pedro as frontmen, Trafficante arranged for the Tropicana to be operated by Harry "Lefty" Clark (aliases: William Gusto, William G. Buschoff, Frank Bischoff), a suspected narcotic trafficker, and his brother, Wilbur of Las Vegas's Desert Inn. His principal assistant in the casino was one Pierre Canavese who had been previously deported from the U.S. to Italy but had subsequently entered Cuba by means of a fraudulent passport and was closely associated with Lucky Luciano

Although Lewis McWillie was officially appointed manager of the casino, the manager-in-chief of all the casinos in Havana was Lansky himself. According to author T.J. English, it was Lansky who knew how to run gambling operations with efficiency and good will. The showgirls at the Tropicana, known collectively as "Las Diosas de Carne" (or "Flesh Goddesses"), were renowned the world over for their voluptuousness, and the cabaret showcased a kind of sequin-and-feather musical theater that would be copied in Paris, New York, and Las Vegas. The lavish shows were staged by Neyra. Headliners included Xavier Cugat, Paul Robeson, Yma Sumac, Carmen Miranda, Nat King Cole, Josephine Baker and Liberace. Heralded as a "Paradise Under the Stars," the Tropicana became known for its showgirls, conga sounds, domino tournaments and flashy, spectacular productions. Nat King Cole's wife Maria paints a colorful portrait of the venue in its heyday: "It was breathtaking! My mouth just fell open...there was so much color, so much movement...and the orchestra! The house band had forty musicians...I said to Nat, 'that's the house band? (Are there) that many showgirls?"

A Cabaret Guide issued in 1956 described The Tropicana as, "the largest and most beautiful night club in the world. Located on what was once a 36,000-square-meter estate, Tropicana has ample room for two complete sets of stages, table areas and dance floors, in addition to well-tended grounds extending beyond the night club proper. Tall trees rising over the tables and through the roof in some spots lend the proper tropical atmosphere which blends well with the ultra-modern architecture of the night club. Shows include a chorus line of 50 and the dancers often perform on catwalks among the trees. Rhythms and costumes are colorfully native, with voodooism a frequent theme. Top talent is imported from abroad. Minimum at tables is $4.50 per person, but this can be avoided by sitting at central bar which has a good view of both stages."

An unpublished article sent to Cuban Information Archives around 1956-57 describes the club in detail, "So as not to waste anyone's time, the gambling room at Tropicana is located right off the entrance lobby. The chandeliered room has ten tables for the usual fun and games, plus 30 slot machines lining the walls. Beyond the gambling room are the nightclub's two dining, dancing and show areas. The two areas are distinct: one is outdoors, with tall royal palms rising among and over the tables; the other is indoors and called the Crystal Arch. The Arch is indeed a huge, modernistic arch-like structure, and this area is used in inclement weather (and also when the outdoor area gets so crowded that there is no more room for customers). Tropicana's total seating capacity: 1,750, but of course you can stand at the bar or at the crap table, and the management won't object at all. Because of Tropicana's bucolic surroundings, the producer of the shows, Rodrigo Neira (better known simply as Rodney), can really spread himself. A Tropicana production number is not complete unless it includes at least half the chorus line dancing on catwalks among the trees. The schoolteacher from Paducah is suitable impressed when he sees scantily clad lassies scampering in front of him, to his right, to his left and above him. This is as hard on the neck muscles as watching a tennis match."

Also in 1956 Martín Fox arranged a special Club Tropicana tourist package: Cubana Airlines' Tropicana Special began a round-trip flight that ferried club customers from Miami to the Tropicana and returned them to Florida at 4am the following morning. The plane featured a wet bar stocked with a bevy of cocktail selections, as well as a scaled-down version of Armando Romeu's orchestra for anyone brave enough to dance in the aisles.

The club soon became "a magnet for international celebrities, musicians, beautiful women, and gangsters.". The long list of stars who flocked to the Tropicana included Édith Piaf, Ernest Hemingway, Jimmy Durante, Pier Angeli, Maurice Chevalier, Sammy Davis, Jr. and Marlon Brando.

The history of the cabaret is detailed in *Tropicana Nights: The Life and Times of the Legendary Cuban Nightclub* (Harcourt, 2005) by Rosa Lowinger and Ofelia Fox. In *Booklist*, Mike Tribby reviewed:

> Lowinger and Fox tell the story of Havana's notorious Tropicana nightclub, the template from which Las Vegas was made after the Batista government collapsed, and the Tropicana was closed. In its day the Tropicana was a prime site for gambling, elegance, seeing and being seen--a resort of choice for international gangsters and jet-setters. Readers who enjoyed Anthony Haden-Guest's "biography" of Studio 54, *The Last Party* (1997), will enjoy comparing the differing modes of showmanship, decadence, and ostentation current in the Tropicana's 1950s heyday to those of 1970s New York's debauched disco scene. Fox married Tropicana owner Martin Fox in 1952 and helped him run it until 1962, when they decamped to Miami. She and Lowinger take pains to establish that the Tropicana was hardly a sleazy Mob hangout but rather a world-class entertainment venue that discriminating gangsters happened to enjoy frequenting. An excellent resource on Cuban popular culture, lavish entertainment, and everyday life just before and just after Castro, this is also an exciting and rewarding read.

The Cuban Revolution was to have serious repercussions for the mob's involvement in Cuba. As early as December 31, 1956 a bomb exploded at The Tropicana. It was set by communist rebels to target the mafia godfathers in Havana. The explosion was contained to the bar area and one woman lost an arm. Despite this, and as even as Castro's rebels began to overthrow Havana two years later, Trafficante was heard to insist that the revolution was, "a temporary storm" that would "blow over." Lansky, the son of

Russian exiles, disagreed. "I know a communist revolution when I see one," he said. He was correct. The new Cuban president, Manuel Urrutia Lleó closed the casinos and nationalized all the casino and hotel properties. This action essentially wiped out both Trafficante and Lansky's asset base and revenue streams in Havana. Cutting his losses Lansky decided to flee Havana. Trafficante remained, hoping he could cut a deal with the new regime. But Castro was not interested. He wanted to make an example of the mob, and Trafficante was seen as someone involved with Batista. He was hunted down and arrested. On June 21, 1959, along with friends of his like Guiseppe di Giorgi and Jack Lansky, Meyer's brother, Trafficante was interned in the Tiscornia camp in Havana.

Martín and his wife Ofelia Suárez, who had no children, fled to Miami. Martín died of a stroke in the mid-1960s. When Ofelia moved to Los Angeles with her long-time companion Rosa Sanchez, her Glendale house became a gathering place and social center for Cuban-American friends and neighbors who continued the Tropicana tradition of domino tournaments. Ofelia died at age 82 on January 2, 2006 of cancer and complications from diabetes at Burbank's Providence St. Joseph Medical Center.

Visiting

The Tropicana continues to operate to this day, attracting tourists to its Cabaret Shows taking place at 9pm, Tuesday to Sunday, in the open-air Salon Bajo Las Estrellas (weather permitting). These days, foreign tour groups comprise the majority of patrons. The layout of the club means that from many of the seats the show is difficult to see, although no seats have a restricted view. Tickets begin at CUC$65.

Gallery

Snapshots from Tropicana Cabaret

See also

- Anacaona
- Buena Vista Social Club

Further reading

- Excerpt from *Tropicana Nights: The Life and Times of the Legendary Cuban Nightclub* by Rosa Lowinger and Ofelia Fox [1]
- *Moon Handbooks: Cuba* (Avalon Travel Publishing, 2007). Detailed travel information for visiting the show.
- *Mi Moto Fidel: Motorcycling Through Castro's Cuba* (National Geographic Adventure Press, 2001). Includes description of the author meeting a Tropicana dancer and their subsequent love affair.

External links

- Andy Carvin/Susanne Cornwall: A Night at the Tropicana [2] - Photos of the show

Industriales

Industriales	
League	Cuban National Series (Occidental Zone)
Location	Havana
Ballpark	Estadio Latinoamericano
Year Founded	1961-62
Nickname(s)	*Los leones* (Lions), *Los azules* (Blues)
League championships	None
Cuban National Series championships	1963, 1964, 1965, 1966, 1973, 1986, 1992, 1996, 2003, 2004, 2006, 2010
2009-10	39-36 (1st, Occidental Zone)
	2009-2010 Champions
Manager	Germán Mesa
Uniforms	
Home	**Away**

Industriales is a baseball team in the Cuban National Series. One of the two teams based in the city of Havana, Industriales is historically the most successful team in the National Series, the main domestic competition in post-revolutionary Cuban baseball. They are similar to the New York Yankees in the sense that they have fans all over the country, being a sure sellout in any stadium, also hated by many outside the capital. The Super Classic of Cuban National Series takes place six times per season between Industriales and Santiago de Cuba, and it's also the equivalent of the MLB classic New York Yankees-Boston Red Sox, the matchup also represents the rivalry between the two cities (La Habana and Santiago de Cuba), dating back to the era when Cuba was a colony of Spain, two centuries ago. They are known as the Lions (*los leones*) or "the Blue Ones" (*los azules*) or "the Blue Lions" (los Leones Azules). Royal blue is their color, though teams like Camagüey and Ciego de Ávila also have blue uniforms (navy blue and sky blue, respectively.)

History

The team was founded in the year 1962, as representatives of all the workers from all the industries of Cuba. Industriales is the perceived heir to the Almendares baseball team from the professional Cuban League. They won the Cuban National Series in 1963, 1964, 1965, 1966, 1973, 1986, 1992, 1996, 2003, 2004, 2006 and 2010. Today the team holds the record of victories in a season (90 games in Cuba) with 66 .

Current roster

- **Catchers**: Alden Mesa, Frank Camilo Morejón, Jockel Gil y Alejandro Regueira
- **Infielders**: Alexander Malleta, Raiko Olivares, Leugim Barroso, Roberto Carlos Ramírez, Rudy Reyes y Juan Carlos Torriente
- **Outfielders**: Carlos Tabares, Yoandry Urgellés, Stayler Hernández y Serguei Pérez
- **Pitchers**: Arleys Sánchez, Yoandri Portal ,Ian Rendón, Deinis Suárez, Frank Montieth, Odrisamer Despaigne, Reinier Roll, Armando Rivero, Yadiel Torres, Ebrys Martínez, César López, Rodolfo Fernández y Ramón Cairoz Jr.

National Series MVPs

The following Industriales players have been named the National Series' most valuable player.

- 1965 Urbano González
- 1967 Pedro Chávez
- 1971 Antonio Jiménez
- 1972 Agustín Marquetti
- 1986 Lázaro Vargas
- 1987 Javier Méndez
- 1996 Jorge Fumero
- 2003 Javier Méndez

Other notable players

- Rey Vicente Anglada (second base)
- Armando Capiró (outfield)
- José Modesto Darcourt (pitcher)
- Ángel Leocadio Díaz (pitcher)
- Antonio González (baseball) (shortstop)
- Ricardo Lazo (catcher)
- Raúl López (pitcher)

- Reinaldo Linares (outfield)
- Santiago "Changa Mederos" Mederos (pitcher)
- Pedro Medina (catcher)
- Germán Mesa (shortstop)
- Eulogio Osorio (outfield)
- Juan Padilla (second base)
- Rodolfo Puente (shortstop)
- Lázaro de la Torre (pitcher)
- Lázaro Valle (pitcher)
- Kendry Morales (pitcher-outfielder-infielder)
- Yasser Gomez (outfielder)
- Orlando "El Duque" Hernandez (pitcher)
- Javier Mendez (outfielder)
- Agustin Marqueti (first baseman)
- Yoandry Urgelles (outfielder)
- Carlos Tabares (centerfielder)
- Yadel Marti (pitcher)

Emigrants

A number of Industriales players have defected from Cuba, often to pursue professional baseball in other countries. These include the following:

- Jesus Ametller
- Ivan Alvarez
- Luis Alvarez Estrada
- Juan Chavez Álvarez
- Leonardo Fariñas
- René Arocha
- Evel Bastida
- Bárbaro Cañizares
- Alexis Cabrejas
- Roberto Colina
- Yunel Escobar
- Osvaldo Fernandez Guerra
- Bárbaro Garbey
- Mario González
- Yamel Guevara
- Adrian Hernández

- Michel Hernández
- Orlando Hernández
- Liván Hernández
- Manuel Hurtado
- Yoan Limonta-Zayas
- Donell Linares
- Agustin Marquetti Jr.
- Ángel Leocadio Díaz
- Kendry Morales
- Vladimir Núñez
- Rey Ordóñez
- William Ortega
- Hassan Peña
- Rolando Pastor
- Mayque Quintero
- Euclides Rojas
- Rolando Viera
- Omar Yapur
- Yadel Marti
- Yasser Gomez

External links

- [1] Official Site

Metropolitanos

Metropolitanos	
League	Cuban National Series (Group A)
Location	Havana
Ballpark	Estadio Latinoamericano
Year Founded	1974-75
Nickname(s)	*Guerreros* (Warriors), Metros
League championships	None
2005-06	19-69 (4th, Group A)
Manager	Juan Padilla
Uniforms	
Home	**Away**

The **Metropolitanos** of Havana is a baseball team in the Cuban National Series. The Metros, also known as the *Guerreros* (Warriors), has historically been a poor team, though it is ostensibly the heir to the Habana teams of the pre-revolutionary Cuban League.

It is one of two teams based in the city of Havana - the other being the more successful Industriales.

Frequently, the National Series removes several of the best players from the Metropolitanos squad and sends them to Industriales. Players including Rene Arocha, Osvaldo Fernández, Frank Montieth and Antonio Scull have begun their careers with the *Guerreros*, only to be sent later to the *Leones*.

Current roster

- **Catchers**: Joquel Gil, Maikel Piñero, Lisván Correa
- **Infielders**: Michel Fors, Wilber de Armas, Yusmani Guerra, Roberto Carlos Ramírez, Leguim Barroso, Ryan Oneil Álvarez, Joice Su, Juan Carlos Torriente
- **Outfielders**: Alexander Barrios, Irait Chirino, Oscar Mesa, Eliú Torres, Starley Hernández, Brian Camacho
- **Pitchers**: Luis Alberto González, Luis Felipe Díaz, René Espín, Heriberto Collazo, Rolando Hernández, Esdiani Puente, José Luis Larrinaga, Yadier Torres, Johan Caballero, Miguel Ángel Rubido, Ebris Martínez, Abel Viego, Rigoberto Arrebato

Notable players

- **Infielders**: Rey Vicente Anglada (second base), Enrique Díaz (second base), Rodolfo Puente (shortstop), Antonio Scull (first base), Rolando Verde (third base)
- **Outfielders**: Armando Capiró, Jorge Salfrán, Oscar Valdés, Bombon Salazar, Julian Villar
- **Catcher**: Iván Correa, Ernudis Poulot
- **Pitchers**: José Modesto Darcourt, Rafael Gómez, Lázaro de la Torre, Ramón Villabrille

Also: Osvaldo Fernández Guerra, Eduardo Rodríguez

Emigrants

- René Arocha
- Osvaldo Fernández Guerra
- Alejandro Zuaznabar

External links

- Unofficial site [1]

Estadio Latinoamericano

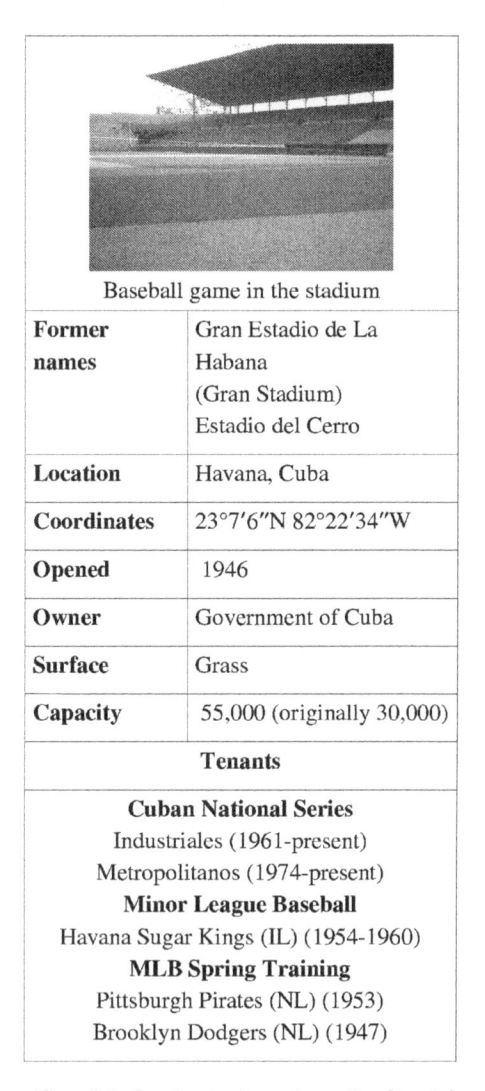

Baseball game in the stadium

Former names	Gran Estadio de La Habana (Gran Stadium) Estadio del Cerro
Location	Havana, Cuba
Coordinates	23°7′6″N 82°22′34″W
Opened	1946
Owner	Government of Cuba
Surface	Grass
Capacity	55,000 (originally 30,000)
Tenants	

Cuban National Series
Industriales (1961-present)
Metropolitanos (1974-present)
Minor League Baseball
Havana Sugar Kings (IL) (1954-1960)
MLB Spring Training
Pittsburgh Pirates (NL) (1953)
Brooklyn Dodgers (NL) (1947)

The **Estadio Latinoamericano** (Spanish for *Latin American Stadium*) is a stadium in Havana, Cuba. It is primarily used for baseball. Gran Stadium, a spacious pitchers' park with prevailing winds blowing in and boasting a playing surface and lighting system of major-league quality, was built in 1946 as the top baseball park in Latin America. Located in the Cerro neighborhood, it opened with the name **Gran Stadium de La Habana** and currently holds about 55,000 people. In 1999, it also hosted an exhibition series between the Cuban National Team and the Baltimore Orioles.

The Estadio Lationoamericano is popularly known in Cuba as "The Colossus of Cerro." Initially it was called *Gran Stadium de La Habana* (Great Stadium of Havana) but later it was called *Estadio del*

Cerro (Stadium of Cerro) until 1961, when it was renamed as Latin-American Stadium when Cuban professional baseball was stopped. It was constructed in 1946 and debuted on October 26 before a crowd of 31,000 fans. It displaced La Tropical Stadium as the best stadium in Havana.

The stadium debuted on October 26, 1946 before a crowd of 31,000 fans for a clash between the Almendares and Cienfuegos baseball teams, the largest crowd that had attended a sports event in Cuba. Almendares won the game 9 to 1. The Venezuelan Alejandro Carrasquel, who in the Major League played for the Washington Senators, threw the first pitch of the game.

In its more than 60 years, the stadium has been utilised for diverse spectacles including popular dance performances and boxing matches.

The stadium was renovated and expanded in the year 1971, with an enlargement of its stands, increasing the stadium to its present capacity of 55,000 spectators, and an extension of its gardens.

The stadium has also been used for political purposes. In 1956 it was the location of a student demonstration headed by José Antonio Echeverría, against the Government of Fulgencio Batista.

Estadio Panamericano, Havana

Estadio Panamericano is a multi-use stadium in Havana, Cuba. It is currently used mostly for football matches and was used as the main stadium for the 1991 Pan American Games. The stadium is able to hold 50,000 people.

Geographical coordinates: 23°9′27″N 82°19′00″W

Estadio Pedro Marrero

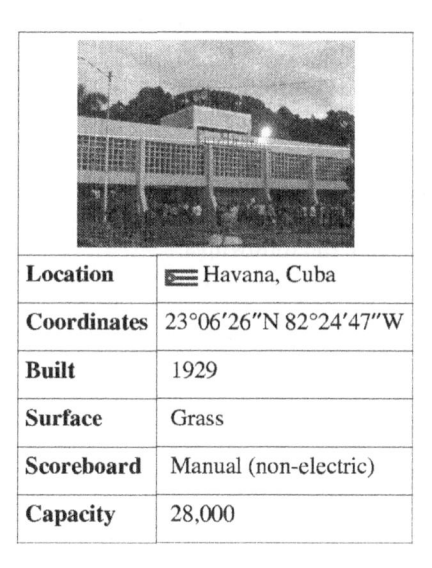

Location	Havana, Cuba
Coordinates	23°06′26″N 82°24′47″W
Built	1929
Surface	Grass
Scoreboard	Manual (non-electric)
Capacity	28,000

Estadio Pedro Marrero, the home of CF Ciudad de La Habana, is a multi-purpose stadium in Havana, Cuba. It is now used primarily for football matches. The stadium holds 28,000 and was built in 1929. Originally named **Gran Stadium Cervecería Tropical** (or familiarly, **La Tropical**), it hosted the 1937 Bacardi Bowl and many Cuban League baseball games. After the revolution, it was renamed for Pedro Marrero, a young man who died in the attack on the Moncada Barracks.

Marabana

Marabana, is the name a popular marathon in Cuba. Since 1987 the Marabana has been held in Havana, Cuba, during the month of November. It contains both a half marathon and a marathon in a circuit around the most central avenues in Havana, starting and finishing in Old Havana.

Technical specifications

Some specifications of the marathon are the followings:

Three different races are held:

- Marathon: 42 195 meters
- Half marathon: 21 097.50 meters
- Mini-marathon por la paz: 4 219 meters

Limit Time:

- Marathon 5 hours
- Half marathon 3 hours

Supply stations are found every 2 kilometers and first aid stations are found every 3 kilometers.

Actual records

Marathon

- Men- 2:13:37
- Women- 2:44:12

Half marathon:

- Men- 1:04:23
- Women- 1:16:16

Subscription Fee

- 50 Cuban Convertible Pesos (Approx. 50 USD)

Winners of the Half Marathon

Year	Male	Female
1987	Alexis Cuba	Emperatriz Wilson
1988	Alberto Cuba	Isabel Arias
1989	Alberto Cuba	Emperatriz Wilson
1990	Ángel Rodríguez	Emperatriz Wilson
1991	Diosdado Matos	Natalia Aróstica
1992	Alberto Cuba	Emperatriz Wilson
1993	Ángel Rodríguez	Emperatriz Wilson
1994	Luis Cadet	Yesenia Centeno
1995	Alexis Cuba	Emperatriz Wilson
1996	Alberto Cuba	Yesenia Centeno
1997	Ángel Rodríguez	Mariela González
1998	Luis Cadet	Mariela González
1999	Hirán Trutié	Mariela González
2000	Aguelmis Rojas	Mariela González
2001	Aguelmis Rojas	Mariela González (CR 1.14:56hrs)
2002	Aguelmis Rojas	Mariela González
2003	Aguelmis Rojas	Mariela González
2004	Norbert Gutiérrez	Yailén García
2005	Aguelmis Rojas (CR 1.03:40hrs)	Mariela González
2006	Norbert Gutiérrez	Mariela González
2007	Aquelmis Rojas	Dailin Belmontes
2008	Norbert Y. Gutiérrez	Yarisleydis Fuentes
2009	Henry Jaen (CR 1.06:16hrs)	Dailin Belmonte (CR 1.18:07hrs)

Winners Marathon

Year	Male	Female
1990	José Ramón Rodríguez	Niurka Cuesta
1991	José Ramón Rodríguez	Isabel Arias
1992	Alejandro Salvador (MEX)	Natalia Aróstica
1993	Marcelino López (MEX)	Anna Sacchi ITA)
1994	Alberto Cuba (CR 2.13:37hrs)	Yesenia Centeno
1995	José Ramón Rodríguez	Fidelina Limonta
1996	Ángel Ferreiro	Sergia Martínez
1997	Freddy López	Adelina Limonta
1998	Alexis Cuba	Yesenia Centeno
1999	Nelson Cabral	Emperatriz Wilson
2000	Luis Cadet	Emperatriz Wilson
2001	Alberto Cuba	Emperatriz Wilson (CR 2.43:40hrs)
2002	Ángel Ferreiro	Zenaida Alonso
2003	Yosbel Arboláez	Emperatriz Wilson
2004	Hirán Trutie	Emperatriz Wilson
2005	Isbel Milián	Aracelys Lamothe
2006	Henry Jaén	Aracelys Lamothe
2007	Henry Jaén (CR 2.29:23hrs)	Mariela Gonzalez (CR 2.51:182hrs)
2008	Aquelmis Rojas (CR 2.20:56hrs)	Daylin Belmonte (CR 2.52:45hrs)
2009	Jorge Suarez (CR 2.27:42hrs)	Liuris M. Figueredo (CR 3.03:23hrs)

External links

- Official Site of Marabana [1]

Transportation

José Martí International Airport

José Martí International Airport Aeropuerto Internacional José Martí	
IATA: HAV – ICAO: MUHA	

José Martí
International Airport

José Martí
International Airport (Cuba)

Summary	
Airport type	Public
Owner	{{{owner}}}
Operator	ECASA S.A.
Serves	Havana
Location	Boyeros Municipality
Hub for	Cubana de Aviación Aerocaribbean
Elevation AMSL	210 ft / 64 m
Coordinates	22°59′20″N 82°24′32″W
Website	www.airportcuba.com/jm [1]

Runways			
Direction	**Length**		**Surface**
	ft	**m**	

06/24	13,123	4,000	Asphalt

José Martí International Airport (IATA: **HAV**, ICAO: **MUHA**), previously called El **Rancho Boyeros International Airport**, is located 15 km (9 mi) southwest of Havana, Cuba, and is a hub for Cubana de Aviación, Aerogaviota and Aerocaribbean, and former Latin American hub for Aeroflot Soviet Airlines. The airport lies in the municipality of Boyeros. It is named in memory of patriot and poet José Martí.

Havana airport is operated by *ECASA* (Empresa Cubana de Aeropuertos y Servicios Aeronáuticos S.A.). It is Cuba's main international and domestic gateway, it serves several million passengers each year, 80% of Cuba's international passengers along with Varadero's Juan Gualberto Gómez Airport.

There are currently three terminals in use at the airport plus an additional terminal operated only by Aerocaribbean.

History

The construction of José Martí Airport was authorized in March 1929. On 24 February 1930, the airport officially opened, replacing *Havana Columbia Airport*. On 30 October 1930, Cubana de Aviación's (at the time CNCAC, S.A.) first ever flight Havana-Santiago de Cuba carried the mail using a Ford trimotor with stops in Santa Clara, Morón and Camaguey. In 1936 non-commercial flights to Madrid started with an Lockheed Sirius aircraft made out of wood lined with cloth, had a Pratt & Whitney Wasp 550 hp (410 kW) engine, a cruising speed of 180 mph and no radio. The aircraft named "4th of September" was commanded by Capt. Antonio Menéndez Pélaez and was flown previously between Camaguey, Cuba and Seville, Spain. By January 1943 the airport had its first control tower and was as well the first control tower in the country. The first commercial international flight out of the airport was flown by Cubana de Aviación's DC-3 Havana-Miami. By 1950 the airport had a second route to Europe, the flight known as "The route of the stars" Havana-Rome operated by a Cubana DC-4.

In 1961 the relations with the United States deteriorated substantially and with the United States embargo against Cuba, airlines from the United States were not permitted to operate regularly scheduled flights to the airport. In the 1990s special charter flights were approved by the US government to operate from Miami to José Martí for Cuban citizens living in the United States that have close relatives in Cuba. Today, various airlines operate non-stop service between Havana and Miami, including American Eagle Airlines, Gulfstream International Airlines, and several others.

Because of Cuba's relationship with the Soviet Union, the airport during the 1970s and 1980s enjoyed the presence of many Eastern Bloc airline companies, Aeroflot, Czech Airlines, Interflug, LOT. The airport has seen its share of tragedies, as many of the older Soviet built jets that Cubana and some of the other communist airlines (such as the Soviet Union's Aeroflot and the East German Interflug) used have crashed either going from or to this airport.

Terminal 2 opened on 15 November 1988 primarily for direct flights to the United States and charter flights. Ten years later on 27 April 1998, the new international terminal 3 was opened by Canada's Prime Minister Jean Chrétien and Cuban President Fidel Castro. The new terminal with three VIP lounges provides many modern facilities and jetways that the former international terminal 1 did not provide.

In 2002, the Air Freight Logistics Enterprise (ELCA S.A.) opened José Martí's first freight terminal, the freight terminal is a joint venture equally shared between the Cargosur company, part of the Iberia group, and Aerovaradero S.A. of Cuba, with an investment of over $2.5 million USD. The goal of this enterprise, the most modern of its kind in this geographical region, is to facilitate and reduce the cost of freight transportation between Europe and the Americas, in aircraft belonging to various companies. The terminal has a 600-Ton capacity, 2,000 cubic meters of space in two refrigeration and freezing chambers alone, with humidity and gas controls.

The airport is home to IBECA. As part of Cubana's renovation strategy, the airline has sought to upgrade its technical support capabilities, and in 2005 IBECA was created. IBECA is a joint venture company 50% owned by Cubana de Aviación and 50% by Iberia Airlines, it deals with the technical maintenance of Western-built aircraft, including all Airbus and Boeing models. It has contracted with various airlines flying to Cuba to provide maintenance and technical support. Annually, it gives technical coverage to more than 5,000 air operations, for more than 30 different airlines, primarity from Europe and the Americas.

International Terminal 3

Presently José Martí Airport is constructing a new automated center of air traffic control which will give its service to the whole region of the FIR assigned to Cuba. The total radarization of FIR was a prior necessary step, this will completely increase the reliability of the air traffic service that Cuba has in the whole region under its control, which is one the major air traffic volume of Latin America as most flights to/from the east coast United States to Central and South America fly over Cuba's air space, with an estimated over 450 controlled flights daily.

Control tower

Accidents and incidents

- "1977 Aeroflot Ilyushin 62 crash" on 27 May killed 68 of the 70 on-board and one person on the ground. At the time the accident was the deadliest aviation accident in Cuba's history. It remains the second deadliest in Cuba's history. One of the victims was José Carlos Schwarz, a poet and musician from Guinea-Bissau.

- On 3 September 1989, a Cubana de Aviación Ilyushin 62M (CU-T1281) on a non-scheduled international passenger flight to Cologne (Cologne Bonn Airport), Germany crashed shortly after take-off. All of the 115 passengers and 11 crew members as well as 45 persons on the ground were killed and the aircraft was written off. One of the persons onboard was Roberto Volponi, son of the writer Paolo Volponi.

- On 31 March 2003, a Blue Panorama Airlines Boeing 767 (EI-CXO) skidded off the main runway 6 in poor weather and gusting winds. No injuries occurred.

- On 3 May 2007, two army recruits hijacked a plane destined for Miami at José Martí International Airport in Havana. The men killed a hostage before being arrested prior to takeoff. It was the first Cuban hijacking attempt reported since the spring of 2003.

Facilities

Terminals

Terminal 1 used to be the main international and domestic terminal building in the airport prior of the opening of terminal 2, and 3-which was constructed in 1998. The terminal is located on the west side of runway 6. It is now used primarily for domestic flights.

Terminal 2 handles mainly schedule charter flights to and from Miami and New York for US residents with special permission from the United States government and Cuban citizens with US visas, the scheduled charters are operated by Gulfstream Air Charters, ABC Charters, Marazul Charters and C & T Charters. The terminal is located on the north side, just in front of runway 24 threshold. It was constructed in the 1988 when the first charter flights after the revolution were opened from Miami. There are bars, bookshops, newsagents, and also a restaurant on the second floor, as well as car rentals in the arrivals area.

Terminal 3 is the main international terminal, it was open in 1998 by Canada's Prime Minister Jean Chrétien and Fidel Castro, and is the largest and most modern. Ticketing and departures are located on the upper level, arrivals and baggage carousels are located on the lower level. There are several car rentals located in the Arrivals Area, the companies represented include Cubanacar, Fenix, Rent a Car, Rex (limousines and luxury cars), Transtur, and Via Rent-a-Car. In terminal 3 all the bars and restaurants are open 24 hours. There are information desks in the Arrivals and Departure areas. A bank, post office and internet are also available in this terminal.

Terminal 5 is mainly used by Aerocaribbean, but Aerotaxi, which is a Cuban based charter airline, is also present. All flights from the United States will temporarily be handled at this terminal due to construction and remodeling at Terminal 2.

Transfer Between Terminals

There is a bus service between the terminals.

Parking

The airport has short-term car parks. Terminal 3 has 750 parking spaces and Terminal 1 & 2 has 500 parking spaces each. All car parks are situated less than 150 meters from the terminals.

Terminals, airlines and destinations

Aeroflot aircraft at Terminal 3

Airlines	Destinations	Terminal
Aero Caribbean	Belize City, Guatemala City, Managua, Santiago de Cuba	5
Aeroflot	Moscow-Sheremetyevo	3
Aerogaviota	Baracoa, Cayo Coco, Cayo Largo del Sur, Cayo Santa María, Holguín, Mérida, Montego Bay, Nassau, Nueva Gerona, Santiago de Cuba, Trinidad, Varadero	1
Aeroméxico	Cancun, Mexico City	3
Aeroméxico Connect	Mérida	3
Air Canada	Toronto-Pearson	3
Air Caraïbes	Pointe-à-Pitre	3
Air Europa	Madrid	3
Air France	Paris-Charles de Gaulle	3
American Airlines	Miami	2

American Eagle	Miami	2
Bahamasair	Nassau	3
Blue Panorama Airlines	Milan-Malpensa, Rome-Fiumicino	3
Cayman Airways	Grand Cayman	3
Condor	Frankfurt	3
Continental Connection operated by Gulfstream International Airlines	Miami	2
Copa Airlines	Panama City	3
Copa Airlines Colombia	Bogotá	3
Corsairfly	Paris-Orly	3
Cubana de Aviación	Baracoa, Bayamo, Camaguey, Cayo Coco, Cayo Largo del Sur, Ciego de Ávila, Cienfuegos, Guantánamo, Holguín, Manzanillo, Moa, Nueva Gerona, Santa Clara, Santiago de Cuba, Varadero, Victoria de las Tunas	1
Cubana de Aviación	Bogotá, Buenos Aires-Ezeiza, Cancún, Caracas, Guatemala City, London-Gatwick, Madrid, Mexico City, Montréal-Trudeau, Nassau, Paris-Orly, San José de Costa Rica, Santo Domingo, Toronto-Pearson **Seasonal** : Santiago de Chile	3
Cubana operated by Aero Caribbean	Cayo Coco, Cayo Largo del Sur, Holguín	1
Iberia	Madrid	3
LAN Airlines	Santiago de Chile	3
Martinair	Amsterdam	3
Sky King	Miami, New York-JFK	2
TAAG Angola Airlines	Luanda, Sal	3
TACA Airlines	Miami	2
TACA operated by Lacsa	San José de Costa Rica	3
TACA Perú	Lima	3
Virgin Atlantic Airways	London-Gatwick	3
Vision Airlines	Miami, New York-JFK	2

Note

- **Note 1:** All flights to the United States are operated as scheduled Special Authority Charters

Cargo airlines

Airlines	Destinations
Aerocaribbean cargo	
Cubana Cargo	
DHL Express	
Flair Airlines	
IBC Airways	
Líneas Aéreas Suramericanas	

Notes

📝 *This article incorporates public domain material from websites or documents [2] of the Air Force Historical Research Agency.*

External links

- José Martí International Airport official website [1] (Spanish)
- Airport information for MUHA [1] at World Aero Data. Data current as of October 2006.
- Cuban Airports [2]
- http://flightaware.com/live/airport/MUHA

Playa Baracoa Airport

Playa Baracoa Airport		
IATA: UPB – ICAO: MUPB		
Summary		
Airport type	Military/Public	
Serves	Havana	
Hub for	{{{hub}}}	
Elevation AMSL	102 ft / 31 m	
Coordinates	23°1′58″N 82°34′46″W	
Runways		
Direction	**Length**	**Surface**
	ft	m	
02/20	7,563	2,305	Asphalt

Playa Baracoa Airport (IATA: **UPB**, ICAO: **MUPB**) is a regional airport west of Havana, Cuba that serves regional flights in Cuba.

Airlines

- Cubana de Aviación (Varadero)
- Aerogaviota (Cayo Largo)

External links

- Airport information for MUPB [1] at World Aero Data. Data current as of October 2006.

Ferrocarriles de Cuba

Ferrocarriles de Cuba (FCC) or **Ferrocarriles Nacionales de Cuba** (English: **National Railway Company of Cuba**), the only railway operating in the Caribbean islands, provides passenger and freight services for Cuba.

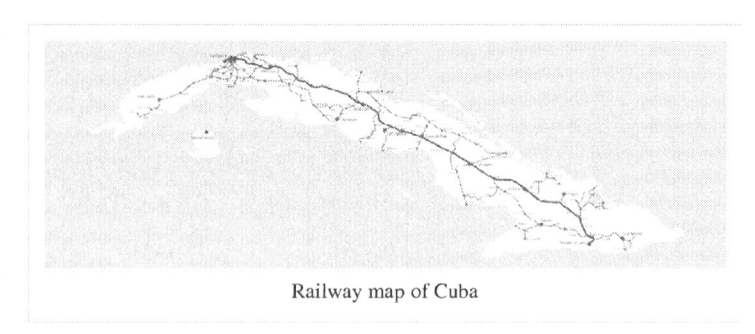

Railway map of Cuba

Route Network

Ferrocarriles de Cuba uses 1435 mm (4 ft 8 $\frac{1}{2}$ in) (standard gauge) that extends from Guane (province Pinar del Río) in the westernmost part of the island up to the bay of Guantánamo in the eastern part.

Most of the 4,226 km is diesel with 140 km electrified. The branch to Trinidad in the south coast is damaged at a bridge and the rail service there is no longer connected to the rest of the national rail network. Local railcars run from the damaged bridge through Trinidad to the coast daily plus a steam locomotive and two home-built coaches on tourist tours through the sugar cane valleys of the Escambray Mountains.

The flagship *Tren Francés* ("French train") travels between Havana and Santiago de Cuba and is operated by coaches originally used in Europe between Paris and Amsterdam on the ex-TEE service. The train is formed by 12 coaches and a Chinese-built diesel locomotive.

The *Hershey Railway* is an electrified railway from Havana to Matanzas that was built by the Hershey Company in order to facilitate transport of workers and products after it had bought sugar plantations in 1916. It is a commuter service running in northern Havana and Matanzas provinces, and some original equipment still exists.

History

Colonial Cuba

In 1836 Gaspar Betancourt Cisneros established a horse drawn railway service called *Ferrocarril de Camaguey a Nuevitas* in Camaguey (Puerto Príncipe).

Cuba's railway history began on October 12, 1834 when the regent queen of Spain Maria Christina of the Two Sicilies approved the building of the first line. When the Compania de Caminos de Hierro de La Habana opened the 27.5 km line from Havana to Bejucal on November 19, 1837, it was the first steam railway line in Latin America. At this point Spain did not possess any railroad lines. The 27.5 km long line from Havana was extended by an additional 17 km to Guines on 19 November 1839. By December 1843 the cities San Felipe and Batabano were added to the rail network and further extensions were added in 1847 (17 km), 1848 (21 km), and 1849 (21 km).

Havana had its first streetcar (Ferrocarril Urbano de la Habana) when its service commenced on 3 February 1859.

Pre-Revolutionary Cuba

American born Canadian railway builder Sir William Van Horne helped expand Cuba's railway network in the early 20th Century. He was an investor in the *Cuba Railroad Company* (founded 1902).

In 1924 **Ferrocarriles Consolidados de Cuba** was created from a dispute between **Ferrocarriles Consolidados de Cuba** and **Ferrocarriles de Cuba**.

Other railway companies would form and merge together in the 1920s:

- Ferrocarriles del Norte de Cuba 1916
- Ferrocarril Espirituano Tunas de Zaza
- Ferrocarril Guantánamo y Occidente

From 1940 to 1959 Cuba's railway system was interrupted by fuel shortage during and after World War II. They were replaced by buses, which transported both passengers and freight

A few sugar factories switched over to diesel electric locomotives to haul freight.

Train ferry

- Prior to the revolution there was a train ferry between Miami and Havana.
- The West India Fruit and Steamship Company was one of a number of companies to provide such service.

Post-Revolutionary Cuba

The destruction of Batista's armoured train by the revolutionaries in the Battle of Santa Clara in December 1958 was an important stepping stone in the Cuban revolution.

After the revolution in 1959, the **Ferrocarriles Nacionales de Cuba** was created by nationalizing the private and public railway systems. MINAZ continued to operate a separate railway system, mainly to transport sugar products.

From 1963 to 1966 British Rail helped the national railway obtain newer locomotives which were based on the Brush Type 4 locomotives at the time being built at Brush Traction in Loughbrough but the final assembly of the Cuban locomotives was performed at Clayton Equipment Company Hatton, Derbyshire.. After the Cuban missile crisis, it became harder for Cuba to buy new railway equipment because of the United States embargo against Cuba. Some trains were delivered via shipment with ships from third countries like Yugoslavia. For example the British locomotive shipped from Hull using Yugoslavian ships.

Purchase of new trains and parts to Cuba with the Western Bloc, stopped from the late 1960s, was replaced through trade with the Eastern Bloc. This trade link collapsed with the fall of the Soviet Union.

Cuba was able to obtain used trains, and even new locomotives, from friendly nations not affected by the embargo:

- 5 Type RSC18 locomotives were shipped from Canada
- 9 electrical motor coaches from Ferrocarrils de la Generalitat de Catalunya (FGC) (Catalonian Government Railways) of Spain

Starting from 2000, the Cuban railway network was improved by more second hand equipment. Larger number now used vehicles were coming from Canada, Mexico and Europe. In 2002 used light rubbing cars (BR771) from Germany.

Much of Cuba's trains are diesel and only a handful are steam locomotives remain for the sugar industry and the tourism industries.

After the 1990s, China became the new supplier of railway cars for Cuba. In 2006, 12 new locomotives (Type DF7G-C at 2500 hp/1900 kW) were shipped to Cuba. China Railways also sold some of their retired cars.

Recent developments

On September 25, 2007, investors from the Venezuelan Bank for Socio-Economic Development (BANDES) reached an agreement with transportation officials in Cuba to invest $100 million for infrastructure improvements and repairs to Cuba's rail network. The work is expected to help increase the average speed of trains on Cuba's railways from 40 km/h (25 mph) to 100 km/h (62 mph). As part of the agreement, Cuban engineers will also work on similar projects on Venezuela's rail network.

In October 2007, the Cuban railways ordered two hundred passenger cars and 550 freight wagons from Iranian manufacturer Wagon Pars.

In May 2010, the Cuban government announced wide-ranging plans to repair the railway network, buy new rolling stock, and open four centres to train railway workers.

Roster

Model	Manufacturer	Numbers	Notes
TE114K diesel locomotives [ru]	Voroshilovgrad Locomotive Factory, USSR	108	
TEM2TK diesel locomotives [ru]	Bryansk Engineering Works [ru], USSR	79	
DVM-9	Ganz, Hungary	70	
MX624 diesel locomotives	MLW, Canada	50	imported in 1976
G8 diesel locomotives	General Motors Electro-Motive Division, USA	51	
TEM4 diesel locomotives	Bryansk Engineering Works [ru], USSR	40	
040-DE	Brissonneau et Lotz, France	42	Similar to French BB 63000 [fr]
TEM15 diesel locomotives	Voroshilovgrad Locomotive Factory, USSR	25	
	General Motors Electro-Motive Division, USA	21	
M62K diesel locomotives	Voroshilovgrad Locomotive Factory, USSR	20	
C30-7 diesel locomotives	GE Transportation Systems, USA	19	
BR 771 railbuses [de]	VEB Waggonbau Bautzen, GDR	17	all sold after 2000
BR 971 [de]	VEB Waggonbau Bautzen, GDR	3	
BR 772 railbuses [de]	VEB Waggonbau Bautzen, GDR	15	
BR 972 [de]	VEB Waggonbau Bautzen, GDR	22	
DF7G-C	CNR Beijing February 7th Locomotive Works , China	47/112	again supplied 2005/2006/2008-2009-2010
DF7K-C	CNR, China	5	First 5 arrived in 2008
GMD1 diesel locomotives	General Motors Electro-Motive Division, Canada	12	From Canadian National Railway to Cuba in 1999

See also

- Transportation in Cuba

References

- Zanetti Lecuona, OSCAR; García Álvarez, Alejandro: Caminos para el azúcar, La Habana: OD. de Ciencias Sociales, 1987.
- Zanetti Lecuona; García Álvarez: Sugar and Railroads. A Cuban History; 1837–1959, Chapel Hill & London: The University OF North Carolina press, 1998.

External links

- Full bus and train timetable [1]
- Information, incl. time table, accessed 2/16/2008 [2]
- Hershey Electric Railroad [3]

Havana Harbor

Havana Harbor is the port of Havana, the capital of Cuba, and it is the main port in Cuba, excluding the US Guantanamo Bay Naval Base (GITMO); technically a territory of the United States, and not a Cuban possession. Most vessels coming to the island make port in Havana; it is where many of the more powerful heads are located.

The Maine

In January 1898 the USS *Maine*, the largest vessel to come out of an American shipyard, was dispatched to Cuba to protect US interests. At the time over 8,000 US citizens resided in the country, and their safety couldn't be assured in the state of affairs at that time. On the fifteenth of February, the Maine was sunk by a mine in the harbor. It became a major rally call for the Spanish-American War, and it caused the US to finally intercede on Cuba's behalf. In 1910 the wreck was removed from the harbor as it was posing a hazard to navigation. It was sunk in deep water in the Gulf of Mexico with proper military ceremonies.

Sources

- http://fcit.usf.edu/Florida/3d/spanam/spanam03.htm
- http://www.history.navy.mil/faqs/faq71-1.htm

Article Sources and Contributors

Havana *Source*: http://en.wikipedia.org/?oldid=389467053 *Contributors*: 1 anonymous edits

Old Havana *Source*: http://en.wikipedia.org/?oldid=381248820 *Contributors*: Hmains

Arroyo Naranjo, Cuba *Source*: http://en.wikipedia.org/?oldid=389574958 *Contributors*:

Boyeros *Source*: http://en.wikipedia.org/?oldid=389094722 *Contributors*:

Santiago de Las Vegas *Source*: http://en.wikipedia.org/?oldid=367523284 *Contributors*:

Centro Habana *Source*: http://en.wikipedia.org/?oldid=389159875 *Contributors*:

Cerro, Cuba *Source*: http://en.wikipedia.org/?oldid=353892140 *Contributors*:

Cotorro, Cuba *Source*: http://en.wikipedia.org/?oldid=368605289 *Contributors*: 1 anonymous edits

Diez de Octubre, Cuba *Source*: http://en.wikipedia.org/?oldid=339399059 *Contributors*: 1 anonymous edits

Guanabacoa *Source*: http://en.wikipedia.org/?oldid=388183064 *Contributors*: 1 anonymous edits

Habana del Este *Source*: http://en.wikipedia.org/?oldid=381891378 *Contributors*: 1 anonymous edits

La Lisa, Cuba *Source*: http://en.wikipedia.org/?oldid=323721878 *Contributors*: Rich Farmbrough

Marianao *Source*: http://en.wikipedia.org/?oldid=380854398 *Contributors*: Hmains

Playa, Havana *Source*: http://en.wikipedia.org/?oldid=366557014 *Contributors*:

Miramar, Havana *Source*: http://en.wikipedia.org/?oldid=383506977 *Contributors*: Iridescent

Plaza de la Revolución *Source*: http://en.wikipedia.org/?oldid=389161784 *Contributors*:

Vedado *Source*: http://en.wikipedia.org/?oldid=339890297 *Contributors*:

Regla *Source*: http://en.wikipedia.org/?oldid=388115326 *Contributors*:

San Miguel del Padrón *Source*: http://en.wikipedia.org/?oldid=388115338 *Contributors*:

Guanabo *Source*: http://en.wikipedia.org/?oldid=366560922 *Contributors*:

Havana Museum of Decorative Arts *Source*: http://en.wikipedia.org/?oldid=304597412 *Contributors*: DerBorg

Museo del Aire (Cuba) *Source*: http://en.wikipedia.org/?oldid=377479047 *Contributors*: Waacstats

Museo Nacional de Bellas Artes de La Habana *Source*: http://en.wikipedia.org/?oldid=389241725 *Contributors*: Look2See1

Museum of the Revolution *Source*: http://en.wikipedia.org/?oldid=389241248 *Contributors*: Look2See1

Real Fabrica de Tabacos Partagás *Source*: http://en.wikipedia.org/?oldid=384571975 *Contributors*: Diuturno

Cathedral of Havana *Source*: http://en.wikipedia.org/?oldid=386369948 *Contributors*: 1 anonymous edits

Basilica Menor de San Francisco de Asis *Source*: http://en.wikipedia.org/?oldid=341482853 *Contributors*: Franklin.vp

Iglesia de Jesús de Miramar *Source*: http://en.wikipedia.org/?oldid=376858198 *Contributors*: Blahma

Beth Shalom Temple (Havana, Cuba) *Source*: http://en.wikipedia.org/?oldid=282481577 *Contributors*: NYC2TLV

Plaza de la Catedral *Source*: http://en.wikipedia.org/?oldid=371302216 *Contributors*:

Palacio de los Capitanes Generales *Source*: http://en.wikipedia.org/?oldid=366470434 *Contributors*:

El Capitolio *Source*: http://en.wikipedia.org/?oldid=389239361 *Contributors*: Look2See1

La Mansion *Source*: http://en.wikipedia.org/?oldid=389241084 *Contributors*: Look2See1

José Martí Memorial *Source*: http://en.wikipedia.org/?oldid=389686314 *Contributors*:

La Cabaña *Source*: http://en.wikipedia.org/?oldid=379622682 *Contributors*: Cordobatim

Castillo de la Real Fuerza *Source*: http://en.wikipedia.org/?oldid=366513979 *Contributors*:

Castillo de San Pedro de la Roca *Source*: http://en.wikipedia.org/?oldid=377264899 *Contributors*:

Morro Castle (fortress) *Source*: http://en.wikipedia.org/?oldid=385225298 *Contributors*: Arjuno3

San Salvador de la Punta Fortress *Source*: http://en.wikipedia.org/?oldid=390048788 *Contributors*:

Colon Cemetery, Havana *Source*: http://en.wikipedia.org/?oldid=381191669 *Contributors*: Colonies Chris

El Templete *Source*: http://en.wikipedia.org/?oldid=389240400 *Contributors*: Look2See1

Christ of Havana *Source*: http://en.wikipedia.org/?oldid=382481155 *Contributors*:

José Martí Anti-Imperialist Plaza *Source*: http://en.wikipedia.org/?oldid=373086421 *Contributors*:

Villa Marista *Source*: http://en.wikipedia.org/?oldid=388973364 *Contributors*: Waacstats

National Symphony Orchestra of Cuba *Source*: http://en.wikipedia.org/?oldid=333497478 *Contributors*:

Great Theatre of Havana *Source*: http://en.wikipedia.org/?oldid=389241424 *Contributors*: Look2See1

National Theater of Cuba *Source*: http://en.wikipedia.org/?oldid=367112265 *Contributors*:

Amadeo Roldán Theater *Source*: http://en.wikipedia.org/?oldid=345212058 *Contributors*:

Gaia (Havana) *Source*: http://en.wikipedia.org/?oldid=379492207 *Contributors*:

Hubert de Blanck Theater *Source*: http://en.wikipedia.org/?oldid=314628105 *Contributors*: Qwerty0

Karl Marx Theater *Source*: http://en.wikipedia.org/?oldid=360737054 *Contributors*:

International Ballet Festival of Havana *Source*: http://en.wikipedia.org/?oldid=367112373 *Contributors*:

Havana Film Festival *Source*: http://en.wikipedia.org/?oldid=373545085 *Contributors*: 1 anonymous edits

Havana's International Book Fair *Source*: http://en.wikipedia.org/?oldid=357103043 *Contributors*:

Havana biennial *Source*: http://en.wikipedia.org/?oldid=390062812 *Contributors*: 1 anonymous edits

Malecón, Havana *Source*: http://en.wikipedia.org/?oldid=353030507 *Contributors*: Navigator4309

Manzana de Gomez *Source*: http://en.wikipedia.org/?oldid=366391220 *Contributors*: Rich Farmbrough

Santa María del Mar, Cuba *Source*: http://en.wikipedia.org/?oldid=335823227 *Contributors*:

Tarara *Source*: http://en.wikipedia.org/?oldid=377876640 *Contributors*: 1 anonymous edits

John Lennon Park *Source*: http://en.wikipedia.org/?oldid=380160306 *Contributors*:

Bodeguita del medio *Source*: http://en.wikipedia.org/?oldid=386875221 *Contributors*: Nicolaspascuzzi

Floridita *Source*: http://en.wikipedia.org/?oldid=387473085 *Contributors*:

Tropicana Club *Source*: http://en.wikipedia.org/?oldid=379183407 *Contributors*: 1 anonymous edits

Industriales *Source*: http://en.wikipedia.org/?oldid=368731224 *Contributors*: Rdubz3000

Metropolitanos *Source*: http://en.wikipedia.org/?oldid=366519646 *Contributors*:

Estadio Latinoamericano *Source*: http://en.wikipedia.org/?oldid=354522941 *Contributors*: 1 anonymous edits

Estadio Panamericano, Havana *Source*: http://en.wikipedia.org/?oldid=381711226 *Contributors*: Spartan008

Estadio Pedro Marrero *Source*: http://en.wikipedia.org/?oldid=386340493 *Contributors*:

Marabana *Source*: http://en.wikipedia.org/?oldid=372526885 *Contributors*:

José Martí International Airport *Source*: http://en.wikipedia.org/?oldid=390227104 *Contributors*: Per aspera ad Astra

Playa Baracoa Airport *Source*: http://en.wikipedia.org/?oldid=305118263 *Contributors*:

Ferrocarriles de Cuba *Source*: http://en.wikipedia.org/?oldid=389936671 *Contributors*:

Havana Harbor *Source*: http://en.wikipedia.org/?oldid=352097305 *Contributors*: Courcelles

Image Sources, Licenses and Contributors

CPSIA information can be obtained at www.ICGtesting.com
Printed in the USA
LVOW02s0105151013

356863LV00012B/652/P